To Karl

[signature] 5/15/02

THE STATE AGAINST RELIGION

THE STATE AGAINST RELIGION

THE CASE FOR EQUAL PROTECTION

Gus R. Stelzer

FOREWORD BY
REVEREND LOUIS P. SHELDON

Acorn Press
Winchester, Virginia

©2001 Gus R. Stelzer

All rights reserved. Reproduction or translation of any part of this work beyond that permitted by Section 107 or 109 of the 1976 United States Copyright Act without the permission of the copyright owner is unlawful. Requests for permission or further information should be addressed to the Permissions Department, Acorn Press.

This publication is designed to provide accurate and authoritative information in regard to the subject matter covered. It is sold with the understanding that the publisher is not engaged in rendering legal, accounting, or other professional service. If legal advice or other expert assistance is required, the services of a competent professional person should be sought. From a Declaration of Principles adopted by a committee of the American Bar Association and a committee of publishers.

Without limiting the rights under copyright reserved above, no part of this publication may be reproduced, stored in or introduced into a retrieval system, or transmitted, in any form or by any means (electronic, mechanical, photocopying, recording, or otherwise) without the prior written permission of both the copyright owner and the above publisher of this book.

Material on pages 66–67, 75–77 is reprinted from *Encyclopedia of Religion in American Politics* by Jeffrey D. Schultz, John G. West, Jr., and Iain Maclean. Copyright © 1999 by The Oryx Press. Used with permission of The Oryx Press, an imprint of Greenwood Publishing Group, Inc., 88 Post Road West, Westport, CT 06881-5007, 800-279-6799, *www.oryxpress.com*

10   9   8   7   6   5   4   3   2   1

Library of Congress Cataloging-in-Publication Data

Stelzer, Gus R., 1915–
    The state against religion : the case for equal protection / by Gus R. Stelzer.
        p. cm.
    Includes index.
    ISBN 1-886939-46-2 (alk. paper)
    1. Religion in the public schools—United States. 2. Church and education—United States. 3. Education and state—United States. I. Title.
    LC111 .S688 2000
    379.2'8'0973—dc21   00-048357

Acorn Press
461 Layside Dr.
Winchester, VA 22602
800-32-BOOKS
Printed in the United States of America

Dedication

This book is written with special acknowledgment to

- ☆ Lorraine, my beautiful and vivacious wife of sixty years, without whom none of this would have been possible,

- ☆ our children Gail and Jack,

- ☆ our grandchildren Laurie, Christine, Carrie, Joan Margaret, John Christopher, Nicholas, and Alexander,

- ☆ and last but not least, our great-grandchildren, little Gus and little Gail.

Thanks for all the joy you added to my life. Now in the twilight of my years, my cup runneth over. May the Lord be as kind to you as He has been to me.

And, may what follows in this book help make it possible for you and all mankind.

Contents

Foreword: Reverend Louis P. Sheldon ☆ ix

Notice ☆ xiii

Chapter 1
A Sad State of Affairs ☆ 1

Chapter 2
The House That Marx and Dewey Built ☆ 21

Chapter 3
America's Biggest Welfare Program ☆ 35

Chapter 4
Adrift in a Moral Vacuum ☆ 49

Chapter 5
The *Humanist Manifesto* ☆ 59

Chapter 6
The First Amendment of the U.S. Constitution ☆ 71

Chapter 7
Putting God Back in the Public Square ☆ 89

Chapter 8
The Economics of Religious Pursuit ☆ 105

Chapter 9
U.S. Supreme Court Fumbles the Football Case ☆ 123

Chapter 10
The Church and State Are Not Separate ☆ 131

Chapter 11
Vouchers—A Case for Equal Protection ☆ 141

In Conclusion ☆ 159

Index ☆ 161

About the Author ☆ 171

Foreword

America has been in a gradual state of moral decline for over four decades—so gradual that most Americans do not sense its totality or its consequences. Like a frog that would promptly jump out if dropped in a pot of boiling water, most Americans would be outraged if the totality of our moral decline were to have been thrust on us in one fell swoop.

But it didn't happen in one fell swoop. It happened gradually, in small increments that were little notice in our busy, pressure-packed lives. We are like another frog that was dropped in a pot of cool water and did not notice the rising temperature of the water until it reached a boiling point, by which time the frog was cooked to death.

So, too, the moral conscience of America has been gradually "cooked" to a point that many people seem unable to sense the degradation that surrounds us . . . or they have surrendered to it in hopeless apathy.

True, many Americans, especially those over fifty years of age, view the sexual revolution as a reflection of that moral decline. Yet they seem at a loss on how to effectively cope with rampant sexual promiscuity; high rates of pregnancies out of wedlock, especially among teenagers; marital infidelity; lack of commitments; high rates of divorce and their negative impact on children; abortions; the rise of homosexual conduct and the attendant HIV/AIDS epidemic; profane and vulgar language; pornography; obscene art; and other departures from traditional morality.

But the moral decline of our nation is not limited to those departures from time-honored standards. It is rampant in nearly every aspect of our social, economic, financial, and political order. Elected and appointed government officials routinely disregard their oaths to uphold the Constitution of the United States. The judicial branch has trashed that sacred document to a point that it bears little resemblance to what our Founding Fathers had in mind.

Executives of financial institutions and corporations wantonly turn their backs on basic principles of moral ethics. They have no regard for the people or the laws of this or any other nation. They shut down thousands of factories and ravage the lives of millions of people who lose their jobs, their homes, their families, their health . . . even their lives. In doing so, they tear apart the social fabric of our nation while creating the widest gap between the rich and poor in our nation's history. Their motivation is evasion of U.S. laws so as to generate higher profits and greater executive compensation with no concern for the carnage inflicted on our society, nor the burdens placed on taxpayers who are forced to pay for programs to offset that carnage.

As a consequence, America has suffered over $2.6 trillion in trade deficits since 1971. Those deficits, in turn, became the major cause of a $5 trillion rise in our federal debt. The average American family must pay $2,300 a year in higher taxes, and higher consumer prices, just to pay the interest on that debt, which functions as a devious mechanism for transferring the meager wealth of 90 percent of our population to the other 10 percent who own or control 90 percent of our private wealth.

Meanwhile, the solvency of Social Security and Medicare is jeopardized; children go without adequate funds for their education; 40 million citizens lack basic health care; and our transportation, utility, and water systems struggle to cope with increased population. Yet, the majority of our citizenry, including our political, academic, and media leaders, seem unable to sense the immorality of it all.

How and why America fell to such low levels of moral comprehension has received little constructive attention.

Foreword

Now comes a new book, *The State Against Religion: The Case for Equal Protection*, that indicts our public school system for failure in the most important subject of all:

☆ The ability of the graduates to tell the difference between right and wrong in matters of moral distinction. Instead, they have been brainwashed to believe that "all discrimination is wrong . . . there are no moral absolutes . . . don't let anyone tell you what your moral standards should be . . . everything can be rationalized or negotiated . . . and above all, you must be tolerant!"

According to author Gus R. Stelzer, we now have a nation of public school graduates who will "tolerate" anything, including a corrupt political system and a president ranked by a panel of noted historians "dead last in moral authority" among America's forty-one presidents.

Stelzer writes that our federal, state, and local governments have created a "top-down, government-run education system" that derives its funding from taxation on all citizens in a manner that the French economist, Frederic Bastiat, called "legalized theft." It then allocates virtually all those funds to a school system that functions as a giant adversary against all forms of God-fearing religion, and against parents who prefer that their children be taught in an environment of moral and spiritual principles.

He documents that the commonly used phrase, "separation of church and state," is nowhere to be found in the U.S. Constitution. To the contrary, the First Amendment places a limit on what government can do with respect to religion, i.e., it "shall make no law with respect to religion" . . . and every person has an unrestricted right of "free exercise of religion and speech," including in the political realm and in the public square.

He reveals that the core philosophy of our public school system is founded on the *Humanist Manifesto* of John Dewey, as drafted in 1933, which defines Humanism as a religion.

By allocating virtually all education funds to a school system based on the religion of Humanism, while denying parents the right to share in funds that belonged to them in the first place in order to enroll their children in a parochial school, Stelzer contends that the State violates the First Amendment, the equal protection clause of the Fourteenth Amendment, and the Tenth Amendment of the U.S. Constitution.

In the last of eleven chapters, the author advances a strong argument in favor of vouchers with no strings attached. Vouchers would be issued to parents or guardians who would make their own decisions as to which school their children should attend, whether it be public, private secular, or parochial. Should the State deny use of such vouchers at parochial schools, the State would compound its violation of the establishment and free exercise clauses of the First Amendment, as well as the equal protection clause of the Fourteenth Amendment.

In summation, Stelzer writes, "Of what value is a Constitutional guarantee of 'free exercise of religion' when the State takes away all, or any part, of its economic life-blood and uses it to create an economic wall that stands as an adversarial barrier to the fulfillment of that guarantee?"

It is a powerful message that addresses what is arguably the most serious issue confronting our nation: the moral decline of our social, economic, and political order. It is a must read for every American concerned about the future of our nation and our posterity.

I urge you to not only read it but study the significance, and then let your representatives in your State Capitols and in Washington, D.C., know exactly how you feel and what they should do about it.

—Reverend Louis P. Sheldon
Founder and Chairman
Traditional Values Coalition

Notice

This book was not written to make money for the author. All proceeds above costs of production and distribution will be donated to:

Alliance Defense Fund
7819 E. Greenway Road—Suite B
Scottsdale, AZ 85260

Focus on the Family
Dr. James Dobson, President
P.O. Box 444
Colorado Springs, CO 80903

Traditional Values Coalition
Rev. Louis P. Sheldon, Founder and Chairman
P.O. Box 97088
Washington, D.C. 20090

In making this commitment the author understands that none of these organizations has any responsibility for the views and other contents expressed in this book. The author assumes all responsibility.

1

A Sad State of Affairs

For over two decades America has been embroiled in controversies concerning elementary and secondary education. At least since 1971, as America became more entangled in a global economy, much has been said about the poor quality of public education: its curricula, declining scholastic results, class sizes, incompetence of teachers and the inadequacy of their compensation, violence, murders, vandalism, etc.

Academic standards and results in subjects like math, science, writing, grammar, geography, and history are among the worst in the developed world. The purpose of this work is not to spell these problems out in detail. Many others have already done so. The situation is common knowledge.

In spite of mountains of evidence concerning the sad state of affairs in basic scholastics and much hand-wringing, no one is measuring our students in the most important subject of all:

☆ The ability to tell the difference between right and wrong in matters of moral distinctions.

To the contrary, students are told "not to be judgmental. All discrimination is wrong. Don't let anyone tell you what your moral standards should be. There are no moral absolutes, everything is 'relative.' Tolerance is a virtue. Everything can be rationalized or negotiated."

Discrimination

☆ The claim that "all discrimination is wrong" is without merit. Discrimination *is* the proper process for distinguishing right from wrong, excellence from mediocrity, good from evil.
☆ If something is wrong, we have a right, indeed a duty, to discriminate against it.

Some degree of discrimination affects most legislation: laws regarding taxes, smoking, lying, prostitution, building codes, divorce, judicial decisions, journalism, etc. We discriminate every time we vote.

☆ The right to discriminate, including the right to decide with whom we wish to associate, is the essence of a free society.
☆ Take away that right and we have thought police, the kind of mind-control dictatorships that prevailed during Stalin's communist regime in the former Soviet Union and Adolph Hitler's Nazi regime, both of which collapsed in utter ruin at a cost of millions of lives. A free people must retain the right of "freedom of thought, expression, and association," which is to say every free person must retain the right to discriminate.

Where and when did the notion that "all discrimination is wrong" take hold in our society? While it existed in a semi-embryonic state during the civil rights revolution of the 1960s, President Clinton gave the concept center stage soon after he was inaugurated in early 1993 when he sought to legitimize homosexual behavior in the U.S. military forces. In an effort to lend credence to that agenda, Clinton's aides, such as George Stephanopolous, repeatedly said that "because all discrimination is wrong, it is wrong to discriminate against homosexuals."

And so, the notion that "all discrimination is wrong" became the battle cry of the homosexual and lesbian lobby with the active support of President Clinton. It then became a key element in the indoctrination of naïve children in public school classrooms to view homosexuality as a "normal" lifestyle that should not be discriminated against.

Students as young as seven have been exposed to programs like "It's Elementary," in which homosexuality is painted as an "acceptable, alternative lifestyle" even though it is a perversion of natural law (i.e., the very purpose of the biological distinction of the sexes), a culture of disease (including HIV/AIDS and other STDs), a source of unwarranted medical costs at taxpayer expense, and premature death. Indeed, studies by the Centers for Disease Control show that the average age of homosexuals who died as a result of having contracted HIV/AIDS was only firty-five as opposed to an average lifespan of seventy-five for all males. Thus, a case can be made that by encouraging children to pursue a homosexual lifestyle, such programs are tantamount to sentencing children to a premature death.

But these facts do not seem to register in the amoral minds of public school officials. Many have authorized "gay club" meetings in school facilities whereas "Bible study clubs" are denied similar rights. This, of course, flies in the face of the U.S. Constitution, which guarantees "free exercise of religion," whereas not a word in that Constitution grants special or preferred rights to homosexuals. Thus, the aggressive agenda of the homosexual and lesbian lobby rests on the flawed notion that "all discrimination is wrong." At the expense of taxpayer/parents who are strongly opposed to such indoctrination of their children, public schools also support this notion.

The Consequences of Tolerance

Perhaps most demoralizing has been the degree to which tolerance has been taught as a virtue, regardless of how degrading or immoral a behavior may be. Children have been inculcated with the need to be tolerant to a degree that, as adults, they will tolerate almost anything, including a corrupt political system and one of the most immoral, if not the most immoral, president in U.S. history. In this age of tolerance, anything goes. We dare not express a word of criticism lest we be accused of being judgmental or intolerant.

Dr. D. James Kennedy, founder of Coral Ridge Ministries, put it this way: "I have repeatedly said that tolerance is the last virtue of a depraved society. When you have an immoral society that has blatantly, proudly, violated all of the commandments, there is one last virtue they insist upon: tolerance for their immorality. They will not have you condemning what they have done as being wrong, and they have created a whole world construct in which they are no longer the criminal or the villain or the evil person, but you are! And so they call evil good, and good evil. The overwhelming majority of high school students in America believe that. They believe it passionately. They have been thoroughly indoctrinated with that idea."

Voltaire said: "I do not agree with what you said, but I will defend to my death your right to say it." If he could know what is happening in this modern era, he would roll over in his grave.

Children are indoctrinated in sex education, most often

against the desires of their parents, and in a manner that has stimulated sexual promiscuity and intercourse between children as young as the age of ten. They are taught the merits of "safe sex," as though if it is safe it is okay, without regard for a tradition that any sexual relationship outside the bonds of matrimony is immoral with dangerous consequences for its practitioners and our entire social and economic order. Public schools distribute condoms to children without approval or knowledge of parents. It is a moral outrage, but our public school system taught our children not to be "judgmental," with a result that as adults they submit to breaches of morality with hardly a word of protest.

It is not surprising, therefore, that before graduating from high school 75 percent of boys have engaged in sexual intercourse with young girls at least twice, while 50 percent of girls have engaged in sexual intercourse at least once during their school years.

Girls have been taught that, in the event they become pregnant, there is an easy way out: they have a "right" to an abortion under the "pro-choice" gospel, so "go ahead and have fun in the meantime." The notion that "choice" should be exercised *before* engaging in a promiscuous sex act is passé in this new age in which there are no moral absolutes, all discrimination is wrong, and tolerance is a virtue.

As a consequence, the number of teenage pregnancies and abortions has soared to record levels, thereby creating a plethora of social problems for which political leaders have no suitable solutions. This situation, in turn, created a gold mine for abortion doctors, who engage in procedures that violate the Hippocratic Oath, which has served as the ethical foundation for the medical profession for over two thousand years.

It is no surprise, therefore, that whereas Dr. Jack Kervorkian was found guilty of "murder" for injecting a fluid that ended the life of Thomas Youk—who had pleaded with the doctor to take him out of his misery, with approval of his wife and brother, and without compensation—abortion doctors are exempted from similar verdicts as they amass huge fortunes while they snuff out the lives of innocent humans who did not ask for their lives to be ended at a rate of nearly four thousand a day. Such is the twisted mentality of a society that was taught that tolerance is a virtue.

Public Schools Become Shooting Galleries

In more recent years, public schools have been the scene of violence, vandalism, harassment, and shooting rampages in which innocent children have been wantonly murdered and wounded. Within less than a month twelve students and a teacher were shot to death by two students at Columbine High School, in Littleton, Colorado, and five students were injured by a student who fired a gun at random on school property in Atlanta.

What was the reaction in terms of a solution to this madness? Almost 100 percent of the outcry was aimed at new laws to control the sale, ownership, and use of guns. Hardly anyone in authority suggested that the cause might be a breakdown in moral concepts throughout our society, starting in our public schools.

Instead, proposals that the Ten Commandments should be posted in every school were ridiculed, thereby feeding the very moral bankruptcy that has been primarily responsible for these and other crimes against humanity.

They totally disregarded this exchange of correspondence:

Dear God:

How could you allow what happened at Columbine?

(Signed) "Student"

A Sad State of Affairs

Dear Student:

I wasn't allowed in the school.

(Signed) "God"

Thousands of students enter public schools with hidden weapons: guns, knives, pipe bombs, etc. On a pretext of protecting students, public schools have become military zones with armed guards, metal detectors, chain-link fences, etc. The impact on students in general is one of lasting fear and concern . . . surely not an atmosphere conducive to education, study, emotional stability, and character development.

Wrong Questions Don't Elicit Right Answers

William K. Shearer, publisher of *The California Statesman*, had this to say in its May-June 1999 edition:

"In the wake of the massacre . . . at Columbine High School . . . , Congress debated the question: Should religious memorial services for the slain students be permitted on the school grounds?

"Is that the real issue? Look around you. America has reached a state of moral degradation in which respect for life has been displaced by a culture of wanton violence.

"America's traditional moral values have been widely ridiculed in the media, and increasingly abandoned throughout societal institutions, including the schools. Prayer in school, or any other open expression of faith, stand condemned. Respect for life perishes as abortion is substituted for personal responsibility and as the Unibomber in the White House dumps tons of bombs on his perceived foreign enemies, the principal accomplishment of which has been the infliction of indescribable suffering on civilian populations. Meanwhile, the media glamorizes the most degrading acts of barbarity.

"Then, when some awful tragedy occurs, such as the mass killing of students by other students at Columbine High, the same public officials who have banned prayer in schools, and the same glib news media pundits who have ridiculed moral values and religious observance, are actually heard calling on the public to pray for the victims of the monstrous shooting. And the U.S. Senate rises to the occasion to vote 85 to 13 to allow religious services for the slain students on the school grounds.

"But what about the question that really should be asked: 'Why can't Americans have non-denominational prayer in schools, and some emphasis on moral values, when it might influence the conduct of children for good, rather than after a savage atrocity has been committed and it is too late?'

"If prayer is good as a consolation to people in loss, if it is permissible on the school grounds after a tragedy like that at Columbine, why is it not even more permissible beforehand to discourage such monstrous conduct? The anti-prayer politicians and media pundits don't have a satisfactory answer to that question."

The Hollywood Factor

The sad plight of what transpires in our public schools has been a key factor in an entertainment industry that subsequently aided and abetted the further contamination of

A Sad State of Affairs

young, formative minds. Hollywood studios crank out a never-ending stream of movies that are *deliberately and intentionally* laced with obscenities, explicit sex scenes, violence, and disrespect for basic moral principles.

Fifteen years ago, at the urging of my teenage granddaughters, I joined them in a visit to a theater to see the film *Tootsie* in which Dustin Hoffman played the part of a man playing the part of a female. I counted twenty-eight times that the audience broke out in laughter. Every occasion was triggered by an obscenity or sexual innuendo deliberately injected by the producers to titillate young minds. Otherwise, so they say, the movie won't sell.

Today, the screens at our local theaters consist overwhelmingly of R rated movies, containing vile and profane language, explicit and unwarranted sex scenes, and gruesome violence. That is why many people, including yours truly, no longer go to the movies. When I am badgered into doing so against my better judgment, I usually leave the theater before the end of the movie with a promise never to go again. How refreshing it is to view movies of forty years ago, in such television programs as "Nick at Night," when my sense of decency is not continuously assaulted.

Up to about 1965, Hollywood voluntarily honored the Hays code, which set strict standards against explicit sex scenes, profanities, and unnecessary violence. But, with the arrival of Jack Valenti as the new voice of the industry, those restraints were abandoned. In spite of frequent calls for moderation, these departures from decency escalated. The content of motion pictures in theaters and on television has become increasingly sordid, with no evidence of a desire to retreat. Indeed, Jack Valenti constantly defends the motion picture industry by implying that the industry simply reflects real life.

And how did that "real life" come into being? Clearly, the groundwork was laid in our public schools, while Hollywood capitalized on it and extended its degradation.

The Drug Culture

Similarly, the world of alleged "music" has departed from anything that contains a musical theme and respectable lyrics, such as in the work of Chopin, Mozart, Beethoven, Greig, DeBussy, Gershwin, Irving Berlin, Jerome Kern, Rogers and Hammerstein, Sammy Cahn and Cole Porter.

Instead, we are bombarded by the nerve-wracking noise and vulgarities of drug addicts and rock stars like Kurt Cobain, Jimi Hendrix, Jerry Garcia, and Janis Joplin . . . now all deceased but still revered in memoriam. One commentator, after being subjected to more than he could stand, asked, "At what point do their brains dribble out of their ears?"

The mainstream print and air media, once dedicated to journalism, but now the products of an amoral public school system, became the propaganda agents for this assault on our moral consciences and sense of decency. Nearly every major paper devotes more space to movies, television, and other forms of alleged "entertainment" than to constructive news.

Example: When drug addict Kurt Cobain, the leader of the group Nirvana, committed suicide, the *Seattle Post-Intelligencer* ran full-page stories reflecting great sorrow for this "tragic" event and concluded by featuring, in color, a full-page photo of Cobain, so his mind-altered fans could hang it in their rooms. Such is the sad state of the contemporary news media, which is now saturated with the amoral graduates of our public schools.

Skullduggery in Congress and the Boardrooms

Meanwhile, the forces of skullduggery in Congress, the White House, the Judiciary, and the boardrooms of corporations, banks, and investment houses took advantage of the declining ability of society at large to tell the difference between right and wrong. With the help and encouragement of a political order that had lost its moral compass, the corporate and financial world promoted a global economy in which the participants have no respect for the laws or the people of any nation.

Unconstitutional Trade Deals

Political leaders, presidents, senators, and congressmen entered into trade deals (GATT, NAFTA, WTO, MFN-for-China, etc.) that violate the U.S. Constitution, notably the equal protection clause of the Fourteenth Amendment, contrary to their oath to uphold and defend that Constitution. They endorsed policies of blatant double standards in violation of basic principles of moral ethics and the *equal application* of our laws.

Example: Federal laws require employers to pay a minimum wage of $5.15 an hour, plus FICA, Social Security, and other tax burdens. The National Labor Relations Act of 1935 legalized strikes for higher wages and better, but more costly, working conditions. The federal government subsidized strikes by granting tax exemption on dues paid into strike funds. They gave millions of dollars in food stamps to strikers so they could put greater pressure on management to submit to their demands. As a result, average base wages for nonsupervisory workers rose from 50 cents an hour in 1935 to $13.50 by 1998, plus another $6 in fringe benefits and another $2 in payroll taxes, raising total labor costs to $21.50 an hour . . . all the result of government mandates.

One might think an honorable government would protect those who abide by these political mandates against any competitor, whether domestic or foreign, who does not abide by the same laws and their cost consequences. But that is beyond the moral comprehension of our political leaders who engaged in trade deals with other nations that encourage importation of products made in foreign countries where wages are below $1 an hour, often paid to people working in sweatshop conditions.

Clearly, such practices violate basic principles of moral ethics and the rule of law. No other competitive activity would tolerate such double standards. The immorality inherent in such duplicities is compounded by the virtual economic and social holocaust it inflicts on the people of this nation.

Since 1971, these double-dealing policies prompted thousands of U.S. factories to close and move to other countries *for the explicit purpose of evading U.S. laws while still retaining the privilege of selling their foreign-made goods in the U.S. so as to enhance profits, and executive compensation, to virtually obscene levels*. In any honest poker game a player who didn't ante up, but who reached for the jackpot, might lose his arm. But the game of a contrived "global economy" is not honest. It is double-dealing in spades.

In the process, the lives of over 20 million Americans were ravaged. They lost their jobs, their homes, their families, their health, even their lives. Worker wages, after inflation and taxes, fell 20 percent by 1997. Industrial areas were decimated. Our social fabric was torn apart as the polarization between rich and poor reached its widest gap since the Great Depression. Our industrial tax base was sabotaged, causing a 1,250 percent increase in federal debt from $408 billion in 1971 to $5.5 trillion by 1998.

Over 75 percent of that debt is caused by trade policies that violate basic principles of moral ethics and the U.S. Constitution. To finance that debt the federal government then pays over $250 billion a year in interest. That, in turn, results in higher taxes, higher interest rates, and higher consumer prices. As such, this devious economic system functions as an insidious scheme to transfer the meager wealth of the poor and middle class to the 10 percent of our population that already owns or controls 90 percent of our nation's private wealth—who own the "mortgages" on the federal treasury—plus foreigners who are paid over $70 billion a year in interest to finance $1.3 trillion of that debt. In so doing, the gap between rich and poor is steadily widened.

One would think that average Americans would rebel against such immoral and unconstitutional trade policies. Yet their moral conscience has been so dulled that they became part of their own financial and social downfall by surrendering to a fool's-gold fantasy that they can enrich themselves by purchasing imports, rather than products of their own country. But you won't find any admonition of this sort in any public school or in the media, which consists mainly of journalists and editors who are graduates of public schools and who, therefore, can't tell the difference between right and wrong. Everything can be rationalized. Everything must be tolerated.

Because the majority of our social order has been indoctrinated in the amoral philosophies of public education they became the easy prey of financial mandarins who are motivated only by greed and power.

Justice Gone Awry

No commentary on this sad state of affairs can be complete without a few words about the moral meltdown in the arena of jurisprudence. Today, thousands of cases each year are not resolved on the evidence and merits of the case. Instead, they are decided by which side has the most clever attorney and the most money . . . with the help of jury members who cannot tell the difference between right and wrong. Innocent people go to prison while guilty people are acquitted.

Example: By all accounts O. J. Simpson was guilty of murdering his ex-wife and a friend. Yet he was acquitted by a jury after less than twenty-four hours of deliberation as a result of clever distortions and diversions by high-priced lawyers. It was a clear degradation of our justice system. To the credit of the legal system, in a subsequent civil action

Simpson was found guilty and ordered to pay millions of dollars in retribution to the families of the murder victims.

In a similar manner, lawsuits filed by high-priced lawyers, on behalf of consumers, have pursued a "deep pocket" assault on corporations and local governments for alleged complaints that have little, if any, merit. One notorious case involved a woman who filed a multimillion-dollar suit against McDonald's on a charge that the coffee in a cup she was holding between her legs in a moving car was "too hot," thereby causing a spill that blistered her skin. Clearly, it was a case of carelessness by the plaintiff, but a jury awarded her $3 million to be paid by McDonald's. What were members of the jury thinking about?

Less known are countless cases in which auto companies have been found guilty of "product defects," with multimillion-, even multibillion-dollar awards in favor of plaintiffs, when, in fact, the accident was caused by other parties or the recklessness of drivers. Auto companies became "deep pockets" for attorneys who skim off 30 percent to 50 percent of the awards. The fact that these "punitive" awards are passed on to consumers in the form of higher prices is never mentioned in court proceedings. Indeed, judges routinely admonish attorneys that juries should not be "contaminated with matters of economics."

Judicial Hostility to Religion

In the face of the above-enumerated breakdowns in scholastic results and human behavior, judges have routinely banned the posting of the Ten Commandments on public property on a convoluted premise that it would violate "separation of church and state" provisions, even though there is no such statement in the Constitution. This specific issue will be addressed at length in subsequent chapters.

In the meantime, some judicial decisions have gone beyond the bizarre. For example: On August 4, 1999, the New Jersey

Supreme Court, in a unanimous 7–0 decision, came down in favor of homosexuals and against the Boy Scouts of America.

Here we have a religiously oriented organization that, for nearly a century, has developed boys into honorable members of our society . . . good citizens and good parents.

But the court ruled in favor of a homosexual who was removed as a Scout leader when his homosexuality became known. Here was a person who engaged in a lifestyle that violates the very purpose of the biological distinctions between males and females and which has been the primary purveyor of the HIV/AIDS epidemic that caused over four hundred thousand premature deaths in America, and billions of dollars in medical costs. The judges opined that good is evil and evil is good, consistent with the notion that there are no moral absolutes.

The grounds for the court's decision was that it violated a state law against discrimination. Aside from the fact that the law violates freedom-of-association concepts, the irony is that the Court engaged in blatant discrimination in doing so. It discriminated *against* an honorable organization *in favor of* an individual who engages in conduct that violates natural law!

The perverseness of this twisted decision should be evident to every clear-thinking person, yet New Jersey Governor Christine Whitman and the amoral mainstream press—all products of our public school system—hailed it as a victory for "fairness."

Fortunately, on July 1, 2000, the U.S. Supreme Court ruled against the New Jersey court. Writing for a 5–4 majority, Chief Justice William Rehnquist found that the Boy Scouts of America are a private "expressive association; that one of the values it sought to express to young people was to 'be clean in word and deed;' that it did not see homosexual conduct as compatible with that value; and that its right to express and protect this value was covered by the First Amendment, regardless of whether anyone else approved. It is not the role of the courts to reject a group's expressed values because they disagree with those values. The Boy Scouts of America has a right not to be forced to support values with which they do not agree."

The Day America Sold Its Moral Soul

Perhaps no event in recent times documents the decline of moral standards in America more than the unwillingness of the U.S. Senate to convict President Clinton, on February 12, 1999, of crimes documented in the Articles of Impeachment passed by the House of Representatives. On that day America sold its moral soul.

A member of his own party (including his close friend, retired Democratic Senator Dale Bumpers) denounced Clinton's behavior as "disgraceful, immoral, deplorable, reprehensible, sordid, shameful, disgusting, indefensible, etc."

Senator Dianne Feinstein was equally harsh while adding "egregious, lying to the American people, lying to the Cabinet, lying in judicial proceedings," and when he finally fessed up Feinstein said, "my trust in his credibility has been badly shattered." Yet she and all other members of her party voted to acquit Clinton on a specious claim that he has been a "good" president.

That raises a question: On what basis did Feinstein and others conclude that Clinton was a good president? There was no debate in Congress on whether he was a good president based on any standard of goodness. Some inferred that he was responsible for a good economy, but others disagreed with that assumption.

Indeed, some pointed to such Clinton policies as a $250 billion tax increase in 1993 and rising trade deficits that actually eroded the economy. Some said that if any one, or all three, of the Three Stooges had been in the Oval Office the economy would be just as good, if not better. Some implied that if his transgression of moral and civil law should be excused if he was, in fact, responsible for a good economy, then so should a corporate executive be pardoned for price fixing if it makes money for the stockholders.

Clearly, senators who voted for Clinton's acquittal were influenced by polls which indicated that over 60 percent of Americans gave Clinton high marks. Rather than go against what they deemed was voter opinion, and thereby risk losing their favor in the next election, the senators sold their own souls in order to save their own political skins.

Who were the real culprits in this sad scenario? That majority segment of our society who said, in spite of Clinton's disgusting and criminal behaviors, he was a good president.

If such behavior is the mark of good in the minds of a majority of Americans, we have indeed sold our moral souls to the devil.

And so, the sour fruits of our public school system became the final arbiter in this tragic injustice. The mind-control process of public school education, which urged its students to avoid all forms of discrimination, judgmentalism, and intolerance, finally came to roost. As adults, a regrettable majority of our society are so lacking in moral distinctions that they tolerate almost anything, including the moral bankruptcy of their own president.

Bombing to Create a New Legacy

Then, in less than fifty days after his acquittal by the Senate, in a bogus attempt to establish a new legacy as a humanitarian, Clinton launched our military forces into one of the most despicable acts by our government in American history in the form of round-the-clock bombing of Yugoslavia and Kosovo: a nation that posed no threat to our national security, a nation that never engaged in a belligerent act against us.

In doing so, Clinton violated the U.S. Constitution, which says that only Congress can declare war against another nation. Congress did not make that declaration because they had no Constitutional basis for doing so. Our Founding Fathers said that a declaration of war against another nation would be permissible only if that other nation had engaged in a belligerent act against the U.S.

Our first and greatest president, George Washington, said, "I have always given it as my decided opinion, that no nation had a right to intermeddle in the internal concerns of another; that every one had a right to form and adopt whatever government they liked best to live under, themselves."

The claim that Clinton had a right to intervene in Yugoslavia/Kosovo for humanitarian reasons was a fraud designed to cover up the real reasons, one of which was cited by Clinton himself: "If we are going to have a strong economic relationship that includes our ability to sell around the world, Europe has got to be a key. Americans must accept the inevitable logic of globalization and free trade . . . both of which depend on America's overseas military commitments and power."

In another words, Clinton was saying that the unconscionable bombing of innocent people in a faraway nation was all about money and that the primary purpose of our military forces was to protect financial powers and corporations.

But that was not the only excuse. The planned intervention in Yugoslavia and Kosovo, and the demonization of Slobodan Milosevic, were under way before the bombing started in late March. It was being set up even before the Senate acquitted Clinton on February 12, as a way to establish a new legacy for Clinton as a humanitarian, to offset the indignities stemming from his impeachment by the House. It was all a fraud.

Sadly, an amoral populace that was taught in their childhood that judgmentalism and intolerance were wrong didn't have enough moral capacity to see through one of the most shameful acts in American history, one that will keep American troops involved for decades in a part of the world that is none of our business in the first place.

Clinton also violated the U.N. Charter and the NATO

charter, both of which forbid armed aggression against any nation that had not engaged in a belligerent action against other nations.

The bombings destroyed hospitals, residential areas, school buses, bridges, and civilian facilities. Over two thousand innocent men, women, and children were killed. Yet polls showed a majority of Americans approved this unconstitutional war, while members of Congress stood idly by, and some, like Senator John McCain, advocated use of ground troops.

Ironically, presidential candidate Pat Buchanan, who opposed Clinton's illegal, indeed criminal, aggression against a country that posed no threat to America, was vilified by McCain, who as a senator, should have denounced Clinton's actions as a violation of Congress's exclusive right to declare war. Yet our society, steeped in the amoral swamp of non-judgmentalism and tolerance as promulgated by our public education system, sided with McCain against Buchanan.

The Problem Rests with "the People"

In the face of all this, it is incomprehensible that anyone with a moral conscience would still say that Clinton has been a good president. What is their basis for determining what is good or what is evil? Clearly, as a result of the brainwashing that took place in their formative years in public schools they have no moral guideposts to make decisions in such matters.

Dr. James Dobson, president of Focus on the Family, said it best: "Our greatest problem is not in the Oval Office. It is with the people of this land. They have lost their ability to discern the difference between right and wrong."

And, where did they lose that ability? They lost it in our public schools over a period of more than sixty years! It was part of the mind-control strategy of Karl Marx and John Dewey all along.

In the following chapters we will explore how we find ourselves in this sad state of affairs and the best solutions.

2

The House That Marx and Dewey Built

To find out what went wrong in education let's first explode some myths and recognize some facts that are commonly ignored.

On September 23, 1990, Linda Ellerbee, an admitted liberal and syndicated columnist, wrote a piece for the *Seattle Post-Intelligencer* titled, "Helping (?) public schools by taking kids out of them." Her purpose was to bash a plan to give parents vouchers that would allow them to send their children to schools of their choice, including secular and parochial private schools.

She wrote: "Everybody has their favorite parts of the American dream. Mine are the rights of a free press and the right to a free public education." Ellerbee was on reasonably sound ground as regards "rights of a free press" because it and "freedom of speech" are specifically protected in the First Amendment of the U.S. Constitution.

But she was dead wrong in claiming "a right to a *free* public education." She was also quite disingenuous by implying that "free public education" is synonymous with, and on the same level of rights as, a "free press."

Public Education Has No Constitutional Authority

The word "education" is nowhere to be found in the U.S. Constitution, nor is there any inference that the federal government has the authority to establish or support a "public school system."

Article I, Section 1 states: "All legislative Powers herein granted shall be vested in a Congress of the United States, which shall consist of a Senate and House of Representatives."

Article I, Section 8 states: "The Congress shall have the Power to" . . . followed by a listing of eighteen duties and powers. The "power" to establish a Department of Education, to appropriate funds for such a purpose, or to grant a federal department the authority to involve itself in matters of "public education" is not listed among the eighteen powers delegated to Congress.

Moreover, the Tenth Amendment specifically states: "The powers not delegated to the United States by the Constitution, nor prohibited by it to the States, are reserved to the States respectively, or to the people."

Therefore, the federal Department of Education has no standing under the U.S. Constitution. It has no constitutional authority to exist, let alone impose on state and local school systems its coercive powers to say how such local schools should be conducted, class sizes, what should be taught, test standards, or any other function related to education.

Nor does the federal government have constitutional authority to impose taxes on *all* citizens for the purpose of funding a government-run school system, which many parents do not want for their children, to the discriminatory exclusion of other forms of education that many parents *do* want for their children. In other words, the federal government has no authority to be involved in the education of our children.

After the Revolutionary War (the period between 1776 and 1789), when the U.S. Constitution was written and ratified, there was no education "system" at all. What little collective education that did exist was confined to local communities, mostly funded by private groups and religious denominations that sought to further their sectarian needs.

In a 1981 edition of the *U.S. News and World Report*, then-Senator Robert Packwood said: "You often hear that this country was founded on public education, but that is not true. There were no tax-supported public schools in the United States until 1818. Prior to that, most grade schools and high schools were church-run, even though they were open to anyone who wanted to go."

The "right" to a free public education has no more credibility than to claim a "right" to free food stamps, free housing, or a free lunch. Nothing about these freebies is free, and there is not a word in the U.S. Constitution even remotely suggesting such Faustian notions. Indeed, as will be discussed at length herein, the public school system is founded on inherently compulsory practices, including coercive taxation, which is the antithesis of freedom.

The First Amendment

Contrary to Ms. Ellerbee's insinuation, here is what the First Amendment *does* say:

> Congress shall make no law respecting an establishment of religion; or prohibiting the free exercise thereof; or abridging freedom of speech; or of the press; or the

right of the people peaceably to assemble, and to petition the Government for a redress of grievances.

With a clear understanding of these facts, let us now dissect the public education system so we can plainly see what it is. The public school system has four basic characteristics, which will be addressed in detail:

1. Public schools are founded on plunder and legalized theft.
2. Public schools are founded on Karl Marx's *Socialism*, the *Communist Manifesto*, and John Dewey's *Humanist Manifesto*.
3. Public education is America's biggest welfare program.
4. Public schools are adrift in a moral vacuum.

Public Schools are Founded on Plunder and Legalized Theft

In his book, *The Law*, written in 1850, eminent French economist Frederic Bastiat wrote: "Man can satisfy his needs and wants only by the ceaseless application of his faculties to natural resources. That is the origin of all property."

His use of the word "faculties" may be defined as "labor" or "work." His use of the word "property" may be more broadly defined as "income, wealth, higher living standards, savings, and the origin of all tax revenue." In other words, all income, wealth, and tax revenues are created by the labor of people who *earn* it "by the ceaseless application of their faculties," often by the sweat of their brows and aches in their backs.

He then explained that individuals or groups could acquire wealth through "plunder," as in military conquests, piracy, embezzlement, exploitation, confiscation, theft, and, finally, "legalized theft." However, in no such instance is the total wealth of mankind increased. Such methods simply transfer wealth from those who earn and create it to those who engage in various methods of plunder.

Legalized Theft

He further defined "legalized theft" as dictatorial taxation whereby governments confiscate the wealth of those who actually earn it, and then give it to others who did not earn it. This is a sort of Robin Hood process, except that it is not a case of stealing from the rich and giving it to the poor.

- ☆ Instead, it a process of "stealing" money from *everyone* so as to give it to certain interests favored by social engineers and the ruling political elite. Very often it serves to enhance the image of politicians who presume that such "compassion" will earn more votes in upcoming elections and, thus, retain their jobs at taxpayer expense. In other words, they are using a public education monopoly to buy our votes with our own money!
- ☆ Bastiat concluded his remarks on this subject by saying, in effect: Woe be to any nation that resorts to plunder and legalized theft. Little could he have realized how his admonition would become reality in America . . . of all places: "the land of the free."

Legalized Theft in Action

Not a word in the Constitution authorizes Congress, or any other governmental body, to appropriate taxpayer money for public education.

In 1790, the year of the first Congress under the Constitution, total federal, state, and local taxes amounted to less than $6.75 per capita. Today, it is over $10,000 per capita . . . about $30,000 per average household!

In 1790, not a penny of government taxes was allocated to public education. Even as recently as 1960 total expenditures for elementary and secondary public education came to only $15.6 billion, or just $258 per household. Of that amount $700 million, or less than 5 percent, came from the federal treasury.

By 1998 total government taxation for elementary and secondary education had soared to $320 billion, or $3,200 per household, over 12 times greater than in 1960! Of that total, $37 billion, or 12 percent, came from the federal government . . . 53 times more than in 1960!

This reflects not only a huge increase in legalized theft to fund public education, but also a substantial increase in federal involvement in public schools, contrary to a general view that public schools, if any, should be controlled by parents at the local level, in accordance with the Tenth Amendment.

Indoctrination of Children by Government Edict

Along with this huge increase in federal involvement in the funding of local schools came increased involvement in the content of what is taught in local schools, such as the notorious Outcome-Based Education (OBE) and Goals 2000. Little by little, the indoctrination of America's children has been taken over by bureaucrats far removed from local control, without parental awareness of what is really taking place . . . and against the wishes of thousands of teachers and administrators.

- ☆ Government outlays for public education now exceed every other category of expenditure, including Social Security and national defense. Indeed, in 1998 it exceeded outlays for Social Security by 24 percent and national defense by 79 percent.
- ☆ While this fact alone should frighten every parent, the real fear lies in the fact that what takes place in our

schools is part of the mind-control and antireligious agenda of bureaucrats in Washington aimed at destroying the ability of graduates of the public school system to distinguish right from wrong. This, of course, makes them more receptive to political demagoguery for the benefit of special-interest groups.

More Spending Has Not Improved Public Schools

Whereas the National Education Association (NEA) and other teacher unions have consistently complained that teacher salaries are too low, average salaries for K–12 classroom teachers soared from $15,913 in 1960 to $40,133 (for less than ten months of work), a 152 percent increase even as average classroom size dropped from 26.4 in 1960 to only 16.9 in 1998, a 40 percent decline.

And what did this tremendous increase in taxpayer funding and smaller class sizes do for public schools? The short answer is the sad state of affairs got worse, not only as regards what is happening inside the schools, but also the conduct and thought processes of those who graduated and who now, as adults, shape public opinion for more government programs that undermine the liberty for which our forefathers fought.

It should be abundantly clear that when government engages in "legalized theft" to fund any program that violates basic principles of morality and liberty, the end product cannot possibly be in the best interests of We, the People.

Thus, in spite of much hand-wringing about the decline of scholastic standards, and a tremendous increase in federal, state, and local taxpayer funding, public schools have continued to decline in virtually every standard of measurement. Frederic Bastiat's warning, 150 years ago, is now reality.

☆ ☆ ☆

Public Schools Are Founded on Karl Marx's *Socialism*, the *Communist Manifesto*, and John Dewey's *Humanist Manifesto*

Karl Marx Sets the Agenda

In his *Communist Manifesto* of 1848, Karl Marx proclaimed that "the salvation of mankind depends on molding young minds so as to throw off the shackles of capitalism." He said, in effect, that it would take several generations to achieve that goal . . . that it could be achieved only in a gradual process.

His proclamation is consistent with the oft-stated advice on how to cook a frog: "If you throw a live frog into boiling water it will immediately jump out. But if you throw a live frog into cool water it will not resist. As the water is gradually heated to a boiling point the frog will be cooked to death!"

And so it is with respect to public education. If the current socialist, neocommunist, amoral policies of public education were to have been thrust on "We, the People" one hundred years ago in one fell swoop, the people would have revolted and said, "We will have no part of that."

But in the late 1800s, along came John Dewey, the father of public education philosophy as we now know it, to carry out Karl Marx's socialist program. The key was to eliminate any taint of God-fearing religion, which Marx said "is the opium of the masses." Dewey believed in remolding society gradually through "socially organized intelligence and organized social planning."

John Dewey Takes Charge

Such planning began in the classroom, where Dewey worked to downgrade competition among students and to promote "cooperation and harmony." He objected to the traditional atmosphere where children sit in fixed rows of desks and see their teacher as "an instructor and disciplinarian."

Dewey thought it wise to put everyone on the same level, face to face, where they could discuss "cooperative plans for individual and group activity." Instead of teachers "instructing," students were invited to say what "they thought . . . how they felt, etc."

In *School and Society,* published in 1899, Dewey wrote, "It is one of the great mistakes of education to make reading and writing constitute the bulk of the school work in the first two years. The mere absorbing of facts and truths is so exclusively individual an affair that it tends to pass into selfishness. There is no obvious social motive for the acquirement of mere learning. There is no clear social gain. We must shape the minds of our children, so they will yield to the betterment of society. In that way, children, and later as adults, will be more in harmony with the socialist agenda."

Dewey served on the Advisory Council of the Institute of International Education, which sponsored summer schools for American students at the post-revolutionary Communist Moscow University. He was also the vice president of the Communist-controlled American Society for Cultural Relations with Russia.

Dewey Helps Write the Humanist Manifesto

☆ In 1933 Dewey was a principal author of the *Humanist Manifesto* and one of its signers. It called for an end to traditional religion and advocated a religious humanism, which then became the reigning "faith" in America's public schools.

The *Humanist Manifesto* will be reviewed at length in a subsequent chapter. It will then become quite clear that the authors of that document fully intended for "humanism" to be recognized as a "religion" that places its "faith" in nature and humanity. Concurrently humanism rejects any reverence for "God," the "Creator," or any "Supreme Being" . . . and any moral principles espoused by God-fearing religion, such as the Ten Commandments.

The *Humanist Manifesto* is cited here as preliminary notice that it was the philosophy of John Dewey, an atheist, who then projected those philosophies into our public education system. It was at this juncture in American history that public schools, under the influence of John Dewey, became an *adversary* of traditional religions, including Christianity and Judaism.

> ☆ We will then see how our government-run public school system, founded on "religious" philosophies as expressed in the *Humanist Manifesto,* violates the First Amendment, as well as the "equal protection" clause of the Fourteenth Amendment. Moreover, it will then become clear that government, with the full force of its economic powers, has assumed an *adversarial* stance against traditional religions via the "humanist religion" of John Dewey in violation of the U.S. Constitution.

The National Education Association (NEA)

The *Journal* of the National Education Association (NEA) devoted its December 1929 issue to Dewey and made him a lifetime member of the union. In 1949, the NEA made Dewey an honorary president. Beating today's NEA to the punch, Dewey said: "Children who know how to think for themselves spoil the harmony of the collective society which is coming, where everyone is interdependent."

Socialism Breeds Its Own Dire Consequences

It is well documented that nations that embrace socialism, or communism, are inevitably confronted with their predictable dire consequences. The collapse of the Soviet Union and its devastating results are clear testimony. Likewise, the need for Sweden, France, Britain, China, and other countries to release themselves from the chains of socialism has been quite evident.

Socialism, whether it be with respect to education or any other facet of a socioeconomic order, is doomed to failure for the simple reason that it violates Bastiat's law that man can satisfy his wants and needs only by the application of his faculties to natural resources . . . to assume their own responsibilities. Simply stated, there is no free lunch . . . and no one has a right to force anyone else to pay for that lunch.

In this connection it is worth heeding the philosophy of General and President George Washington: "The Parliament of Great Britain have no more right to put their hands into *my* pocket, without my consent, than I have to put my hands into *yours*." While Washington spoke of the "Parliament of Great Britain" the point of his remark is just as applicable to our own federal and state legislatures.

Responsibilities

It follows, therefore, that men and women who are not ready and willing to assume full personal responsibility for themselves and their own children, including their education, should not engage in a sex act that may bring a child into this world. Failure to honor this basic principle must be viewed as a breach of moral ethics, if not a "crime" worse than the offenses committed by many now incarcerated in our prisons.

The *gradual* retardation of young minds, and their *gradual* declining ability to tell right from wrong, has encouraged more and more people to look to government for their own salvation, and that of their children.

But, of course, government cannot accommodate those demands unless it first puts its hands in the pockets of those who actually earned their money by the ceaseless application of their faculties in a disciplined lifestyle on a premise that it is up to every individual to assume their own responsibilities, including the education and care of their children.

Unfortunately, as more Americans departed from the principles of liberty embodied in the Declaration of Independence, as a result of their indoctrination into socialism by our public school system, as envisioned by Marx and Dewey, they defaulted on their own responsibilities while demanding that government put its hands in the pockets of others to make up for their lack of personal responsibility. In that manner, they and their children have become wards of the state.

The Fallacy of Child Care

An insidious byproduct of this progression toward socialism has been the growing tendency of parents to be less involved in other aspects of child rearing. Having transferred responsibility for the education of their children to government schools (via legalized theft), they also assume that schools should assume responsibilities beyond education of their children.

Teachers and administrators are now asked to function as counselors and virtual child-sitters to offset the dysfunctional environment in many households where parents spend far too little time in providing the in-home educational and emotional support children need from the time they enter this world. That's the way it was for thousands of years before Marx and Dewey.

Indeed, this phenomenon has advanced to a point where parents are demanding that government provide for child care and the funds to place their children under the care of paid workers, including subsidizing the wages of child-care workers. This departure from time-honored parental responsibilities is another sad chapter in the history of Marx/Dewey socialism as promoted in our government-run public school system. Nothing can take the place of parents with respect to child care, especially in the first five years.

Adverse Impact of U.S. Economic Policies

While these are the undesirable results of public school education, we should not overlook the part played by U.S. trade, immigration, and monetary policies, which are deliberately formulated to provide a ready pool of cheap labor, whether it be within U.S. borders, or the products of cheap labor in foreign countries, that constitute a de facto violation of U.S. labor laws.

Since the end of World War II American workers have been pitted against the lowest wage and living standards in the world under the fraudulent idol of free trade in a global economy. Keep in mind that Karl Marx, during a speech in Brussels in 1848, said that he favored "free trade" because it hastens the social revolution, thereby creating *global socialism.*

Since 1971 over 20 million Americans lost their jobs as a result of global socialism, euphemistically called a "global economy," with free trade as its operating agenda. Real inflation-adjusted wages, after taxes, fell by 20 percent. This has been exacerbated by high rates of legal and illegal immigration from low-wage countries, and a monetary policy based on maintaining inordinately high rates of unemployment and underutilization of the productive faculties of U.S. workers.

This *planned* economic squeeze has caused family disorders by the millions: endless bickering between parents (mostly over money problems), divorce, and the need for both parents to work, leaving millions of children without adequate parental guidance and support, thereby placing more burdens on teachers and school administrators.

But it should not be the responsibility of public educators to offset the social problems caused by economic policies deliberately designed to keep 80 percent of our population in a virtual state of servitude and constant economic quandary. The economic policies of our government have created a virtual "dog-eat-dog" society in which the headmaster is greed, without responsibility for the social carnage the society generates.

(This subject was dealt with, in great length, in my previous book, *The Nightmare of Camelot*, which came off the presses in December 1994. That book revealed why U.S. trade and economic policies are immoral, unconstitutional, and economic demagoguery. So I shall not pursue this vital matter in this work, which is devoted to education.)

The Public Education System Is Bankrupt

Taxpayers are forced to pay increasingly higher taxes to fund an education system that is incapable of coping with a society in which 80 percent are in a virtual state of semifinancial bankruptcy at the same time that it is morally bankrupt. There is no more reason to expect that this failed system will produce desired results than it is reasonable to expect pigs to fly.

Rev. E. Ray Moore, a South Carolina pastor, put it another way: "I think government education can't be reformed. It's like teaching a pig to dance. It never works, you get dirty, and the pig gets mad."

Stay tuned.

3

America's Biggest Welfare Program

Chapter 2 identified four elements that make up America's public education system. The third element identified the public education system as the biggest welfare program in America. This chapter will document that indictment.

It is generally understood that AFDC (Aid for Dependent Children) is one of America's many welfare programs. So are food stamps, housing aid, legal aid, unemployment aid, Medicaid, income tax credits, among others.

Each of these government programs, at taxpayer expense, fills a void that people are unable or unwilling to fill.

If people cannot afford to pay rent or are unwilling to do the necessary things to afford housing, government steps in with housing aid. If they cannot afford food, government provides food stamps. If they cannot afford an attorney, government provides legal aid. If people cannot afford basic medical services, government provides Medicaid, etc., etc.

We take all of that for granted . . . as part of the Great Welfare Society launched by Lyndon Baines Johnson soon after assuming residency in the White House in November 1963.

Yet, for some strange reason when parents are unable, or unwilling, to pay for the education of their children, and government fills the void with "free" public schools, no one seems to think of it as welfare.

Free Public Schools Are Not Free

At $320 billion a year just for elementary and secondary schools, education is not only America's biggest welfare program, it is bigger than all other welfare programs *combined*! And when government spends another $150 billion in confiscated taxes for higher education, bringing total "aid" for public education to $470 billion, still no one thinks of it as welfare.

But that is what it is . . . welfare! It is welfare caused by parental inability or unwillingness to pay for the education of their own children. So a system has been devised, and expanded, to confiscate money from everyone to pay for the education of children of parents who are unable, or unwilling, to assume their own responsibilities.

In many cases, that aid (I'm trying not to call it welfare, again) is not for just one child, but two, three, four and as many as six or seven children . . . all going to public schools at the expense of taxpayers, many of whom have no children of their own, or who assume the costs of educating their children at private schools, thereby reducing the tax burden on other people.

Adding insult to injury, we find single moms, still in their early twenties, with as many as three or four children born out of wedlock, with no father at home, dipping into these education welfare funds. Yet hardly anyone is heard to condemn such situations. Instead, they are apt to shed "compassionate" tears for the mother and children.

Consider a family with four children and a household income of $40,000 a year . . . slightly above average. They would pay, at best, $2,000 a year in tax funds allocated to schools. Their children attend public schools at a cost of more than $5,000 each or $20,000 a year. Multiply that by 13 years from kindergarten through high school for each child and it adds up to $260,000! In those same 13 years they paid, at best, $26,000 in school taxes, leaving government to "reach into the pockets" of others to make up the difference of $234,000! Now, that *is* welfare any way we care to slice it!

Yet, that is not all. Welfarism is so deeply entrenched in our public education system that it is extended to over one hundred thousand children of illegal aliens who entered the United States in violation of our immigration laws, and who attend our public schools at a cost of millions of dollars to taxpayers.

When former California Governor Pete Wilson demanded that federal immigration authorities send these children, and their parents, back to the countries from whence they emigrated, or compensate the California State treasury for the costs of educating them, he was given the cold shoulder. Neither the National Education Association or the California Teachers' Association came to Wilson's defense, suggesting that these powerful bodies are more interested in feathering their own nests and expanding their political power than in doing the right thing.

A Question of Responsibility

All of these facts raise a question that may offend some people, but a question that must be asked:

- ☆ Why would a man and a woman engage in a sex act that might result in bringing another child into this world unless they are willing and able to provide all the nourishment, guidance, development, and education every child deserves?

Disregard for that obligation must be viewed as one of the most irresponsible acts that can be performed by any man or woman. And, when other people are forced to offset that irresponsibility by a process Bastiat called "legalized plunder," the irresponsibility and immorality of it all is compounded. There is a point at which "compassion" in a socialistic system must face up to reality.

Now, if that happens once, it might be excused, especially if unforeseen circumstances, such as the loss of a job or an incapacitating injury, make it impossible for parents to pay for the education of their child. But, when parents have two, or as many as four or six children, without being able or willing to pay for the education of even one child, something is seriously wrong with our social policies. Government is condoning and encouraging dereliction of personal responsibilities.

In my own case, my wife and I had two children. The first was born more than two years after we were married, and was conceived only after I was already established in a promising career. We delayed having a second child for another four years until we were certain that we could assume all responsibilities for two children, including education. I did not feel comfortable with the idea of "reaching into anyone else's pockets" to make up for any shortcomings, or lack of personal responsibility, on my part.

Being born into a poor family, my formal education was limited to eight grades in a parochial school. I was forced to go to work to help support my family, consisting of a father who was unemployed most of the time, my mother, four sisters, and a brother. In 1930, at age fourteen, at ten dollars a week, I was the only wage earner in a family of eight.

From that humble beginning I rose to senior executive in the world's largest corporation with responsibility for over one thousand dealers, thirty-five thousand employees, and $2 billion in annual sales before retiring in 1976.

My success was not due to being academically smarter. Instead, I give credit to the good fortune of having been immersed, as a schoolboy, in the moral principles of the Ten Commandments, which guided me throughout life. Those principles enabled me to gain a reputation in a competitive, rough-and-tumble industry for honesty and moral integrity in all my dealings and relationships. That, in turn, earned the full support of subordinates, dealers, and other business associates, leading to record sales, market penetration, and profits . . . with the added plus of sixty years of wedded bliss without ever a thought of straying from my marriage vows.

Both of our children went on to graduate schools and we paid for all of it at private (mostly parochial) schools, except for one year when, as a result of a transfer to another city, we could not find a parochial school in which to enroll our son.

I mention my experience not to boast, but to suggest there is such a thing as morals and personal responsibility . . . that parents should assume their full responsibilities or they should not have children, at least not beyond the first one . . . they should not be trying to assume these responsibilities by reaching into the pockets of others.

Government Encourages Lack of Responsibility

☆ By subsidizing so-called "free" public education, via the "legalized plunder" of someone else's hard-earned money, government encourages lack of responsibility and discipline.

☆ Public education is Marxist socialism and welfarism to the highest degree! It is unfair to children . . . and in the long run to our entire social order. Having been immersed in the amoral swamp of public education, with limited ability, if any, to distinguish right from wrong, students become ill-equipped, as adults, to play a constructive role in a morally right socioeconomic order!

This brings us back to Linda Ellerbee's views about rights.

It begs another question:

- ☆ What "right" does anyone have to invoke the dictatorial arm of government to confiscate the hard-earned money of anyone else in a process Bastiat called "legalized plunder," in order to make up for their own irresponsibility?

I've read the Declaration of Independence and the United States Constitution many times, but have never observed even a tinge of such "rights" in either document. The only documents in which such concepts are implied are the *Communist Manifesto* of Karl Marx and the *Humanist Manifesto* of John Dewey et al.

Primary Beneficiaries of Public Education

Before leaving these thoughts on public education as a welfare program, it is proper to raise another question:

- ☆ Who are the primary beneficiaries of the public education system, including higher education?

It should come as no surprise: The primary beneficiaries are the millions who depend on tax funds for all or most of their income. It includes teachers, professors, associate teachers and professors, administrators, staff personnel, custodians, guards, suppliers of textbooks, computer equipment and other school supplies, etc.

And, of course, it includes the National Education Association (NEA) and dozens of other unions and associations who are forever seeking more tax money for their education monopoly, via "legalized plunder."

None of these people originate or create wealth in a free market. All are dependent on the dictatorial arm of government to confiscate the income of people who actually earn it in the competitive world without benefit of disbursements from tax funds. Indeed, through their unions, they have consistently opposed any semblance of competition in the arena of education, such as tuition tax credits or vouchers, so parents can send their children to the school of their choice, including private secular or parochial schools.

Ungrateful "Tax-Dippers"

One might think that this army of "tax-dippers" would be forever grateful to those who work in the real world of competition, without benefit of tax subsidies, and who are the true generators of real wealth and tax revenue . . . the geese that lay the golden eggs for the benefit of those who depend on tax outlays for their livelihood.

One might think that those who depend on tax outlays for their livelihood would support the people who make those tax funds possible by purchasing the products of their labor. But the records show that a high percentage purchase imports that are made under conditions contrary to virtually every American law, and which contribute nothing to public school funds from which their own livelihood is derived.

Indeed, studies have shown that members of the public education industry are less prone to support American private industries with their tax-initiated consumer dollars than those who work in the competitive world of real private endeavor. With such a low level of moral integrity in public schools it is not surprising that its students reflect declining levels of morality while in school, and later on when, as adults, they contribute to the declining morality of our society at large.

Imports Don't Create Revenue for Public Schools

In 1982, I conducted an intensive survey of cars, not over five years old, owned by the faculty and administrators of 48 elementary and secondary schools, plus two state universities, in

San Diego County. Out of 942 cars, 61 percent bore the nameplate of a foreign manufacturer vs. a national average of only 22 percent. Forty-nine percent were made in Japan and the balance came from West Germany, France, Italy, Britain, and Sweden, all of whom granted tax rebates to their auto producers if they exported their cars to the U.S., with the approval of Congress and the Executive Branch!

Not one of those cars created tax revenue for state or local schools. U.S. taxes on imported cars were limited to a 2 percent tariff on declared customs values, all of which entered the federal treasury . . . none to state or local treasuries.

> ☆ It never seemed to dawn on these school personnel that employees of foreign companies don't pay property, school district, or any other kind of taxes in America. In contrast, cars produced in America generate at least 45 percent of their values in direct taxes (income, property, school district, FICA, etc.) . . . and nearly 100 percent via the ripple multiplier effect for state and local agencies, as well as for the federal government.

One might think that people who work in the field of education would have sufficient intelligence, if not a sense of moral obligation, to buy cars made by American workers who *do* pay taxes into school funds, if for no reason other than to maintain their own jobs and paychecks, and the fact that they are supposed to *educate* their students. But that did not appear to enter the minds of an inordinate percentage of their members who constantly beat the drums for higher salaries and budgets from tax treasuries.

The U.S. vs. Japan

I then spent two days in the Los Angeles office of the Japanese Consulate where I learned the intimate details of the Japanese education system. In Japan, teachers with 15 years' experience were paid $11,300 annually, whereas teachers in the San Diego K–12 Unified School District were paid an average of $23,400. Japanese teachers were required to conduct classes 5.5 hours a day for 240 days a year (three hours on Saturday), vs. only five hours a day for 177 days a year in San Diego. Japanese law required an average of forty students per classroom teacher for the classroom to qualify for funds from the national treasury, compared to an average of only thirty students per classroom teacher in San Diego County.

The bottom line for all of these numbers was that teacher salaries per student/classroom hour were only 21.4 cents in Japan vs. 88.1 cents in San Diego . . . over four times higher!

Qualified observers acknowledged that average seventeen-year-old graduates of Japanese secondary schools were better able to assume a productive role in society than average twenty-two-year-old U.S. college graduates. In summary, Japanese teachers cost much less than in the U.S., and they produced a far better product.

A Challenge to Public School Teachers

I reported my findings in a commentary titled "Import Schools from Japan, too," which appeared in the editorial pages of the *San Diego Union* on September 29, 1982 (see reproduction at the end of this chapter). The article ended with these words:

> "If California teachers and administrators (who now buy the bulk of their cars, TV sets, etc., from Japan) will support American products and workers, I will lead a drive for higher school budgets. But until then maybe we should make our education purchase decisions just like school personnel do, and import our education system from Japan."

Within hours after that edition hit the streets my telephone started ringing and didn't stop for two weeks, including calls at 2 A.M.

Not one member of the public education establishment accepted my offer to lead a drive for higher teacher salaries if they promised to buy American products. All were outraged by my audacity! Calls in the middle of the night elicited no voices, only heavy breathing.

Such is the moral vacuum in which live an inordinately high number of those who are commissioned, at the expense of taxpayers at large, to teach our children. Since many public school personnel themselves are adrift in a moral vacuum, it is no wonder that a regrettably high percentage of graduates of our public school system cannot distinguish right from wrong either. Not only have they not been taught simple economics, they have been given no moral standards to guide them. Instead, students have been led to believe that there are no moral absolutes, everything can be rationalized, everything is relative, and everything can be negotiated.

What Others Had to Say

Over twenty years ago, Dr. Frank E. Fortkamp, who distinguished himself in a long teaching career in high schools and colleges, wrote about the absence of choice in education:

> "Surrendering our schools to the government is surrender to socialism. The essence of socialism is the closed loop of government control. What sense does it make to educate our children in the virtually socialist public education system when these same children must grow up, find jobs and function in a capitalist free enterprise system?
>
> "The rigidity, mediocrity and stultifying conformity of public schools may be maddening, but they are not

surprising. These are the traits inherent in any government operation, and they are to be expected."

English philosopher John Stuart Mill, in his treatise *On Liberty,* written in 1859, saw the dangers all too clearly:

> "A general state education is a mere contrivance for moulding people to be exactly like one another; and as the mould in which it casts them is that which pleases the predominant power in government, whether this be a monarch, a priesthood, an aristocracy, or the majority of the existing generation, it establishes a despotism over the mind, leading by natural tendency to one over the body.
>
> "As one people after another have ignored the warning, despotism has been their lot. The state school system has become a cardinal feature of every totalitarian regime."

Over thirty years ago, the constitutional scholar Dan Smoot spelled it out in his October 10, 1966, report:

> "We will solve our major education problems when the people elect governors, state legislators, Congressmen, and a President who have the courage and good sense to say: 'How dare a government, professing to be free, lay violent hands on children and force them to attend particular schools, study particular books, under particular teachers?'
>
> "Whence does government derive the right to take advantage of my children and say when, where, what, and by whom they shall be taught? Whence does government derive the right to seize another man's money for the education of my children? How dare a government,

professing to be free, invade the domain of private duty and private right that God assigned to parents?"

To which I add, unless the stranglehold the vast army of tax-dippers has on our educational system is eliminated, public education is beyond redemption. It cannot get better. It can only get worse. That is the predictable result of all socialist and communist systems.

The past is prologue.

Commentary

[Originally published in *The San Diego Union*, Sept. 29, 1982, p. B-7]

Import Schools from Japan, Too

By Gus K. Stelzer

Much has been said about California's school budget crises and alleged low teacher salaries. Concurrently, U.S. auto and other factory workers are maligned for wages 70 percent higher than Japanese, who are said to turn out questionably better products. So, it seems only fair to also compare U.S. education standards with Japan.

In Japan, a 40-year-old teacher with more than 15 years' experience is paid $11,300 annually, whereas teachers in the San Diego Unified School District, grades K–12, are paid an average of $23,400 or 106 percent more than a top-flight teacher in Japan.

Japanese teachers conduct classes an average of 5.5 hours for 240 days a year (including 3 hours on Saturday) vs. only 177 days at 5 hours per day in San Diego. The Japanese teacher works 1,320 hours and earns $8.56 per classroom hour, while the average San Diego teacher works only 885 classroom hours at $26.45 each—over three times greater.

America's Biggest Welfare Problem

Japanese law provides for 40 students per teacher, whereas California law limits class size to only 32, and actual experience, under an even more restrictive union contract, is under 30.

The bottom line is: Teacher salary cost per "student-classroom hour" is only 21.4 cents in Japan, vs. 88.1 cents in San Diego—over four times higher! It is safe to assume costs throughout California are similar.

Qualified observers tell us average 17-year-old graduates of Japanese secondary schools are better able to assume a productive role in society than average 22-year-old U.S. college graduates.

Adding further irony, our "protected" public education industry blocks all attempt to grant freedom of choice as to how education dollars are spent (e.g., vouchers, tuition credits, etc.) while it insists on reserving for itself freedom to decide to which country they will send their tax-initiated consumer dollars.

Having foisted on American industry a relatively inferior student product at three to four times the cost, when compared with Japan, it is proper to question the merit of California school demands for higher budgets and salaries, which would be subsequently impacted (via taxes) in the cost of American products, making them even more vulnerable to Japanese imports, which benefit from a better student/employee product at far lower costs.

If California teachers and administrators (who now buy the bulk of their cars, TV sets, etc., from Japan) will support American products and workers, I will lead a drive for higher school budgets. But until then maybe we should make our education purchase decisions just like school personnel do, and import our education system from Japan.

—Stelzer is a resident of Rancho Santa Fe.

4

Adrift in a Moral Vacuum

We now come to the fourth element of America's public school system, i.e., "Public schools are adrift in a moral vacuum."

The amoral graduates of public schools in prior generations have now visited themselves on the current generation in the form of politicians, bureaucrats, public school administrators, faculty, students, parents, and last but not least, a good part of our society.

With increasing emphasis during the past fifty years, students have been indoctrinated into a culture of situation ethics—do whatever it takes to satisfy one's desires in any given situation—while being warned against being discriminatory, judgmental, or intolerant.

All of this activity is in accordance with the humanist philosophy of John Dewey, who said: "Children must be conditioned, through gradual indoctrination, to reject the thought processes transmitted by their parents and churches, so they may be prepared for the new world social order."

It is no wonder, therefore, that there has been a growing lack of respect for a political system that is a mirror reflection of a society shaped by a government education system that lost its way between right and wrong. More and more people have surrendered to a feeling of hopelessness . . . that any effort to reinstill honesty, decency, and moral principles in our political process is an exercise in futility.

Liberal Judges Overrule the Will of the People

Examples are rampant:

Under Initiative 167, Californians voted overwhelmingly to stop the use of confiscated tax dollars to pay for the education and medical care of illegal aliens who violated our immigration laws. Clearly, such practices are wrong if we assume there is such a thing as right and wrong. But a single judge ruled against the wishes of millions who said such misuse of tax funds should be stopped, and a liberal state governor (Gray Davis) refused to challenge that opinion in the Court of Appeals. Two people canceled out the votes of millions of right-thinking people.

In Colorado, citizens overwhelmingly approved Amendment 2, which said no branch of government could force private businesses or property owners to employ or yield to homosexuals. But, in a split decision, five liberal judges on the U.S. Supreme Court voted against that Amendment, while four other judges voted for it. By that narrow margin the Supreme Court struck down Amendment 2 against the wishes of the people of Colorado.

It was the difference of just one judge who canceled out the wishes of hundreds of thousands in Colorado. Justice

Antonin Scalia said, "The majority opinion finds no support in the U.S. Constitution."

On June 29, 1999, the U.S. House of Representatives, by a vote of 275 against and 140 for, rejected Resolution 94 that would have established a national day of prayer. Yet in that same month, President Clinton declared the *entire month* to be a "Gay Pride" month in honor of homosexuals and lesbians, and no one in authority raised a dissenting voice.

Has our national conscience sunk so low that those who pervert natural law, as well as biblical teachings, deserve higher respect than our Creator? Sad to say, it would seem that way.

In July 1985 the Supreme Court ruled that public school teachers may not conduct classes in parochial schools. By a bare majority of 5-to-4, again the difference of just one judge, the court reflected its hostility toward religion and the First Amendment. Writing for the majority, liberal Justice William Brennan wrote that the practice "threatens to convey a message of state support for religion to students and to the general public."

He also said the practice was "an excessive entanglement between church and state." Obviously, Brennan chose to disregard the fact that the state had already "entangled" itself in the matter of "church and state" by confiscating money from religiously oriented parents and using that money to fund a government-run school system that functions as an adversary against parochial schools. Surely, he cannot say that such "plundering" of parental earnings to the detriment of religiously oriented education is not a factor. But he chose to disregard that.

In a dissenting opinion, Justice Sandra Day O'Connor said "the decision is tragic." Chief Justice Warren Burger said the decision "borders on paranoia and exhibits nothing less than hostility toward religion and the children who attend church-sponsored schools."

Growing Apathy

The declining percentage of people who vote in most elections reflects a growing apathy and a feeling of hopelessness.

There is a common view that our two-party political system is corrupt and insensitive to the wishes of the majority. Letters to politicians are not answered. If they are, the response totally evades the issues or questions raised. Attempts to form alternative political parties are rebuffed, ridiculed and scorned by the established political order and its propaganda agents in the liberal socialist media.

It should be no surprise, therefore, that in the short span of 30 years (1967 to 1997), as our political system caved in to the Marx/Dewey socialist/humanist agenda, our federal government piled up a legacy of unconscionable debt for ourselves and our children seventeen times greater than was accumulated in the 177 years from the formation of our Republic in 1789 to 1967!

Yet our citizenry at large, as a result of being dumbed down in our educational system, seems unable to comprehend how this unconscionable debt is the result of global socialism run amok—how it has polarized our society between rich and poor to its widest gap in our history—let alone visualize and support any responsible effort to take corrective action.

Instead, the products of our amoral government educational system prefer to devote their time to mind-altering rock music, R-rated movies, television, sports events, gambling, soap operas, titillating novels, Woodstock, Stonewall, a six-pack of beer, drugs, parties, all in the image of the "bread and circuses" of the Roman era. They resort to almost anything to get their minds off the rot, the malignant cancer that is eating away at our entire social order.

We have become so mired in the swamp of "legalized plunder" that we seem unable to sense the immorality of it all and how our government school system (including higher education) is its fertile breeding ground. After all, what should we expect when our children, beginning at the tender of age of five, are brought up in a socialistic, valueless environment that warns them against being judgmental or intolerant, implying that they should put up with just about anything? Those who dare to be politically incorrect are subjected to vilification, slander, lies, ridicule, discharge, lawsuits, fines, and even imprisonment.

At the same time, we are told that Christians are "right-wing extremists," that "freedom *of* religion" has been superseded by "freedom *from* religion," that sodomy is now okay and we must not oppose it for fear of being called "bigots," that abortions and condoms are now proper antidotes for irresponsible sex acts, that profanities and obscenities are acceptable forms of speech that must be protected under the U.S. Constitution, that even the most disgusting and irresponsible forms of "artistic expression" are protected by the Constitution, that adultery is a way of life, that half-truths and downright lies are okay if they achieve personal goals, that the American Civil Liberties Union has higher legal rights than religiously oriented people, that the Constitution of the United States must surrender to a New World Order in which the modus operandi is fraudulent free-trade ideology, and that "if it is not illegal there is nothing wrong with it."

Sexual Degradation

If the preceding list is not sufficient evidence of the moral decay spawned by our government education system, consider this:

Promiscuous sex and pregnancies are rampant among students. In an amoral attempt to stem this degrading tide, public schools are passing out condoms to teenagers on a premise that sexual intercourse between adolescents is okay as long as it "safe," thereby giving boys even more incentive to "score" on young girls, while girls lose their own self-esteem.

In Lakeside, California, a group of high school students called "Spur Posse" kept "score" on the number of girls they "scored on." One claimed to be the champion, having "scored on" sixty-eight girls. Several others came close. The leaders in this "sporting event" were held up as macho guys in the press and were invited to appear on national television, where they were given the opportunity to brag about their accomplishments with little criticism from their interviewers. It was all in "good fun."

Our moral standards have sunk so low that it is now common practice for men and women to "live and sleep" together outside the bonds of matrimony with hardly a peep from anyone against such lifestyles. Even eyebrows are no longer raised. If and when they do marry, they are unwilling to live up to their vows, leading to record rates of divorce that adversely affect them for the rest of their lives. Of even greater concern is the emotional scars inflicted on their children . . . scars that remain with them the rest of their lives to the detriment of our entire society.

The New World Order

Millions of American consumers, indoctrinated into the New World Order, have become enablers of a global economy/free-trade fraud on a false premise that they are better off to buy products made in other countries than in America. Their sense of moral standards has been reduced to such a level that they are unable to relate their buying decisions to a $5 trillion increase in federal debt between 1971 and 1998 . . . and even less able to comprehend the debilitating effect of that debt.

None of this is to say that other factors have not played a part in the moral decline of our society, but there can be no doubt that our government education system provided the breeding ground and a dominant role in this tragedy.

Linda Bowles Had It Right

Linda Bowles is one of my favorite writers because she is invariably right on every subject. She has a subconscious ability to distinguish right from wrong. With the permission of Linda Bowles, let me share with you some of her comments from a nationally syndicated column in August 1999:

"There are two primary reasons (for the failures of public education):

"First, the federal government has progressively increased its control over the education of American children. It is unconstitutional if one assumes that the 'States rights provision' of the Tenth Amendment to the Constitution is still in place . . . and that Supreme Court justices know how to read.

"It is dangerous for the federal government to get involved in decisions about what *values* should be instilled in children and what *values* should be withheld from them. Government cannot resist the temptation to insert its political agenda into the school curriculum.

"The second reason is government unions, in particular teachers' unions. The growth of educational unions correlates almost perfectly with the decline in the quality, and increase in the cost, of public education.

"The largest and most powerful union in America, the National Education Association (NEA), has struck a Faustian deal with liberal politicians in Congress and the White House. The deal is this: In exchange for millions of dollars of campaign contributions, they get across-the-board support from all their candidates and propagation of all their policies and agendas inside and outside the classroom.

"But let's be fair. While it is true that a good case could be made that we are on the verge of being overrun by an avalanche of ignorance, it would not be entirely fair to say our kids are graduating empty-headed. Perhaps it's time for an updated review of some of the things our children have learned in government school classrooms:

"While Johnny and Jill may not be learning how to read, they are learning that:

— Teachers are underpaid
— God is irrelevant
— Big business is ruining the environment
— Rewards should be based on need rather than performance
— Bisexuals are under the command of unstable genes
— The Alamo was a great Mexican victory
— Society rather than the individual is responsible for crime
— Teachers are quite underpaid
— Thomas Jefferson was a racist
— Two plus two equals whatever
— Competition is destructive
— The right to be wrong makes wrong right
— All rules and standards are mutable
— God is a homophobe
— Porpoises are smarter than people
— The Constitution requires the government to censor religious speech
— Taxes are the same as charitable contributions
— Boys and girls are exactly the same except for unimportant differences

Adrift in a Moral Vacuum

- It is loving to approve or reinforce the wrong in others
- George Washington was a racist
- Rich people enjoy stomping on poor people
- The condom is mightier than the conscience
- Columbus infected the natives with syphilis
- One person's opinion is as good as any other
- The American Constitution was written by racists and sexists
- Teachers are grossly underpaid
- Sex between consenting children is inevitable
- All sexual orientations are created equal
- Religious people are bigots
- In the beginning there was a big explosion
- Trees are important because money grows on them
- The right to kill unborn babies is in the Constitution
- It is un-American to have more than someone else
- It is the Constitutional responsibility of government to provide jobs, housing, clothing, condoms, hot lunches and medical care to all citizens

"Entire generations of children have been indoctrinated into mind-sets that resonate with hedonistic socialism. When these children come of age, what choices will they make? When they assume positions of leadership, how will they change America?

"The well-publicized 1983 report, 'A Nation at Risk,' concluded with this dire statement: The educational foundations of our society are presently being eroded by a rising tide of mediocrity that threatens our very future as a nation and a people."

That is the path we are on today, with no strong consensus that we need to change directions. It is abundantly clear, by virtually every academic and moral standard, that our government education system has failed . . . and that it continues to fail in spite of (or perhaps because of) hundreds of billions of dollars in increased spending.

> ☆ It is the natural consequence of a system founded on Karl Marx socialism and John Dewey Humanism . . . a system adrift in a moral vacuum.

As such, the system is beyond redemption. No amount of fine tuning with more money can fix it because it is broken beyond repair. We've been down that road far too long.

Satisfactory solutions will not be found in the conflicted rhetoric of the public school advocates who are largely responsible. It's like leaving it up to the fox to restore order in a chicken coop after he has had his fill of drumsticks and wings in the midst of flying feathers.

Instead, it means listening to people who are not part of the problem, and who offer new concepts based on sound moral principles.

It means going back to the drawing board with a clean slate and abandoning the monopolistic grip of government school unions. It means allowing every parent the "right," and a realistic opportunity, to send their children to the school of their choice, whether it be public, private secular, or parochial.

Contrary to what Linda Ellerbee said, that choice is the "right" of every parent, as envisioned by our Founding Fathers who so brilliantly wrote the Declaration of Independence and the Constitution of the United States.

5

The *Humanist Manifesto*

John Dewey, The "Father" of Public Schools

In chapter 2 you were introduced to John Dewey, the "father" of public school philosophy as we know it today. Dewey, of course, was an atheist who had no use for God-fearing religions. He believed the universe was brought about by natural evolution and that Earth's inhabitants are the products of natural evolution, even though no credible scientific evidence supports such views. (Evolutionists have never satisfactorily answered the question, "How did it all start?") Dewey believed that mankind should rely on its own resources, abilities, and motivations to achieve its goals without reliance on, or reverence for, any Supreme Being.

By 1899 he was an influential voice in our public schools. By the early 1930s his philosophies had taken a strong foothold in the philosophies and curricula of our public school system.

Humanists Form an Alliance with Public Schools

In 1933, Dewey collaborated with about thirty other atheists to write the *Humanist Manifesto*, which ultimately became the core philosophy of public schools. Therefore, we need to study the *Manifesto*, to see what it says and what its philosophy is. Only then can we understand how the proponents of that *Manifesto* and the leaders of our government-run schools have joined together in an alliance that functions as a giant adversary against all traditional religions that believe in a Supreme Being.

As a result of this strategy, we can then see why traditional religions have been superseded by a new "religion" called "Humanism," which became the core philosophy of our public school system to the exclusion of all God-fearing religions. We can also better understand how the U.S. Constitution has been so grossly misinterpreted by the courts, by politicians, by the media, by corporations, and by a large segment of our population.

With this background, we will be able to understand why there is now such great animosity and hostility against, and a lack of tolerance for, the major religion in America, i.e., Christianity. We will also comprehend more clearly the animosity and hostility regarding strict interpretation of the U.S. Constitution and the religious beliefs and motivations of the men who crafted that document and its amendments in 1787 and 1789.

Humanists Work Behind a Cloak of Secrecy

In writing this book, I hoped to include the complete text of the *Humanist Manifesto*, as written and published in 1933, so that every reader could know exactly what it says and, thus, be able to make their own informed decisions as to its true meaning and significance.

Unfortunately, the American Humanist Association, which holds a copyright to that document, was not willing to grant permission to reprint it in this volume.

The fact that the American Humanist Association was not willing to allow the *Humanist Manifesto* to be revealed verbatim in this book, and to be subjected to critical analysis, should be a matter of great concern to every American who values transparency, the right of every American to have access to information that vitally affects our socioeconomic order, and the ability to relate that *Manifesto* to the documents on which the United States of America was founded.

Consequently, I am limited to my own interpretation and paraphrasing of certain salient statements in the *Humanist Manifesto*. Anyone can obtain a copy of the *Humanist Manifesto* as written in 1933, as well as *Manifesto II* written in 1973, by contacting:

The American Humanist Association
7 Harwood Drive, P.O. Box 1188
Amherst, NY 14226-1788
Phone: (800) 743-6646 or (716) 839-5080
Fax: (716) 839-5079

Or on the Internet, visit http://www/humanist.net/documents.

Humanism Is Defined as a "Religion"

Humanism is described and defined as a "religion" at least thirteen times in the *Humanist Manifesto*. For example, the *Manifesto* makes the following assertions:

> ☆ "In order that religious humanism may be better understood, we, the undersigned, desire to make certain affirmations. . . ."

- ☆ "Religious humanists regard the universe as self-existing and not created."
- ☆ "Religious humanism considers the complete realization of human personality to be the end of man's life and seeks its development in the here and now."
- ☆ "In the place of the old attitudes involved in worship and prayer the humanist finds his religious emotions expressed in a heightened sense of personal life."
- ☆ "Religious humanism maintains that all associations and institutions exist for the fulfillment of human life."

These and other assertions make it clear that humanists themselves claim that Humanism is a religion while simultaneously denying the existence of "God" or any other Supreme Being. Suffice it to say that the above-cited statements from the *Manifesto* are only a sample of its numerous assertions to support the self-proclaimed religion of Humanism.

Humanist claims are in direct opposition to the Declaration of Independence, the sacred document by which the thirteen original colonies liberated themselves from the tyranny of Great Britain. In the Declaration of Independence, Thomas Jefferson paid homage to a Supreme Being in such phrases as: "the Laws of Nature and of Nature's *God* . . . we hold these Truths to be self-evident that all Men are endowed by their *Creator* with certain unalienable rights . . . And for the support of this Declaration, with firm Reliance on the Protection of *Divine Providence*, we mutually pledge to each other our Lives, our Fortunes and our sacred Honor" (emphasis added).

I must wonder what Mr. Jefferson would now say about the manner in which the *Humanist Manifesto* has led to the banning of his "Declaration" in our public schools because it dares to show reverence to "God," our "Creator," and to a "Divine Providence."

The Humanist agenda—and the manner in which it is promoted in our courts, in our political order, in the media, and in our public schools—is diametrically opposed to the handiwork of the fifty-five men who met in Philadelphia in 1787 to craft the Constitution of the United States and its subsequent Bill of Rights. These writings, not the *Humanist Manifesto*, are what our nation is founded on . . . and they are the deliberate work of men who placed their faith and trust in God.

As a result of the gradual indoctrination—over a period of more than sixty years—of the religion of Humanism in the minds of naïve children as they attended our public schools and universities, its secular graduates have made a virtual shambles of the letter and intent of the U.S. Constitution.

Aiding and abetting that agenda was Humanist John Dunphy in the January/February 1983 edition of The American Humanist Association's principal journal, *The Humanist:*

> " . . . the battle for humankind's future must be waged and won in the public school classroom by teachers who . . . perceive their role as proselytizers of a new faith: a religion of humanity that recognizes and respects . . . what theologians call divinity in every human being. These teachers must embody the same selfless dedication as the most rabid fundamentalist preachers. For they will be ministers of another sort, utilizing a classroom instead of a pulpit to convey humanist values in whatever subject they teach. . . .

Humanism Contains No Moral Guideposts

In the religion of Humanism, there are no moral absolutes. Everything can be rationalized and negotiated. In the humanist's mind, ethics and morality can be tailored or manipulated to whatever the situation warrants. Thus, we have "situation ethics," in which most anything goes.

The Humanist's pulpit is a public school system (from

Head Start to universities) funded by nearly $500 billion confiscated from the taxpayers at large in a process that Bastiat called "legalized theft." It is no wonder, therefore, that the Humanist agenda has crept into and distorted our entire judicial system—including our federal and state courts and the U.S. Supreme Court—in one convoluted and immoral ruling after another.

Whereas the Constitution and the Bill of Rights were written to guarantee freedom *of* God-fearing religions, our government-run schools promote the religion of Humanism, which advocates freedom *from* God-fearing religions and their moral principles. The consequences for our entire social, economic, and political order are devastating. Surely, I need not spell out or list the overwhelming evidence. Just listen to the radio or look any day at our newspapers, magazines, and motion picture and television screens.

If current events do not provide conclusive evidence of the immoral swamp in which we are now mired, we need only be reminded that the anti-God, Humanist philosophies of Hitler, Stalin, and Mao produced the greatest human disasters and bloodshed in the entire history of mankind.

The Religion of Humanism

A mature analysis of what has been said thus far may be summarized by stressing certain points, which should be self-evident, about the *Humanist Manifesto,* and its implementation:

1. Humanism rejects traditional religions, such as Christianity, Judaism, etc., that place their "faith" in a Supreme Being.

2. Humanism is a religion and is so recognized no less than thirteen times in the *Humanist Manifesto.*

The *Humanist Manifesto*

3. Humanism is a religion that places its faith in the "here and now" and a belief that man alone is responsible for the realization of his own goals and destinies.

4. Religious Humanism assumes an adversarial stance against traditional religions.

5. John Dewey collaborated in the drafting of *Humanist Manifesto* at the same time that he was highly instrumental in shaping the philosophies of our public school system.

6. The opinions and thought underlying the *Humanist Manifesto* became the core philosophy of America's public schools.

7. America's public school system has adopted the religion of Humanism while simultaneously evicting any semblance of God-fearing religions, contrary to the "free exercise of religion" clause in the First Amendment.

8. The religion of Humanism is totally void of any moral guideposts such as those contained in most traditional religions. Humanism panders to a philosophy that all individuals should decide for themselves what is right and what is wrong.

9. The religion of Humanism promulgates no moral absolutes. Everything can be rationalized within a "heightened sense of personal life" and the stipulation that "there will be no uniquely religious emotions or attitudes of the kind hitherto associated with belief in the supernatural." The proper ethic or moral standard depends on the situation.

John Dewey Linked Humanism and Public Schools

John Dewey, one of the drafters of the *Humanist Manifesto*, was lauded in the *Journal of the National Education Association* (NEA) in its December 1929 edition, and was subsequently made a lifetime member of that union. Then in 1949, sixteen years after Dewey helped write the *Humanist Manifesto*, the NEA made Dewey its honorary president. These actions of the NEA must be viewed as de facto evidence of the extent to which the Humanist views of John Dewey became the core philosophy of our public education system. John Dewey forged the bridge that linked the *Humanist Manifesto* to America's public schools and universities with the ongoing help of the NEA, the ACLU, PAW (People for the American Way), Americans United for Separation of Church and State, etc.

Evolution of Humanism

Statements below are reprinted from page 223 of the *Encyclopedia of Religion in American Politics*. Copyright © 1999 by The Oryx Press, used with permission.

> "Secular Humanism has its . . . roots in the Renaissance . . . when . . . increased emphasis was placed on humans . . . . Although the early form of Humanism . . . stressed the study of ancient Greek and Roman . . . philosophy, it was not hostile to Christianity.
>
> "Modern Humanism has broken that tie with Christianity. . . . The most dramatic . . . statement of American secular humanism was the 1933 *Humanist Manifesto* issued by . . . prominent university professors, including John Dewey.

" ... More recently, the debate over humanism has centered on public schools, where critics of secular humanism say that its dominance is undercutting the moral values of children, and, ultimately, of the United States."

What Qualifies as a Religion?

These comments with respect to what qualifies as a religion are from *West's Encyclopedia of American Law*, volume 8, West Group, 1998, page 303. Copyright © 1998 by WEST GROUP. Reprinted by permission of The Gale Group.

"To determine whether an action of the federal or state government infringes upon a person's right to freedom of religion, the court must decide what qualifies as religion or religious activities for the purposes of the First Amendment. The Supreme Court has interpreted religion to mean a sincere and meaningful belief that occupies in the life of its possessor a place parallel to the place held by God in the lives of other persons. The religion or religious concept need not include belief in the existence of God or a supreme being to be within the scope of the First Amendment.

"As the case of *United States v. Ballard* . . . (1944) . . . demonstrates, the Supreme Court must look to the sincerity of a person's beliefs to help decide if those beliefs constitute a religion that deserves constitutional protection.

"In addition, a belief does not need to be stated in traditional terms to fall within First Amendment protection. For example, Scientology—a system of beliefs that a human being is essentially a free and immortal spirit who merely inhabits a body—does not propound the existence of a supreme being, but it qualifies as a religion under the broad definition propounded by the Supreme Court. The Supreme Court has deliberately avoided establishing an exact or a narrow definition of religion because freedom of religion is a dynamic guarantee that was written in a manner to ensure flexibility and responsiveness to the passage of time and the development of the United States. Thus, religion is not limited to traditional denominations."

Definitions of "Religion"

Adding weight to the *Humanist Manifesto*'s acknowledgment that Humanism is a religion, *Webster's Dictionary* defines religion, in part, as: "Any specific system of belief, worship, conduct, etc.; often involving a code of ethics or philosophy; loosely, any system of beliefs, practices, ethical values, etc.; any subject of conscientious regard and pursuit; as cleanliness was a 'religion' to him."

Finally, and most significantly, in the 1961 Supreme Court case no. 367 U.S. 488, *Torcaso v. Watkins*, Justice Hugo Black, writing for the majority, included this comment:

> "Among religions in the country which do not teach what would generally be considered a belief in the existence of God are Buddhism, Taoism, Ethical Culture, Secular Humanism, and others."

Thus, the Supreme Court, in a majority decision, agreed with contentions contained in the *Humanist Manifesto* that Humanism is a religion.

It is not uncommon, therefore, that some people, like Linda Ellerbee and members of the National Education Association (NEA), believe in the "sanctity" of public education and its ties to the philosophies of John Dewey, to a point that it is a "religion" in their minds.

Another Point of View

In 1986, Bertram F. Collins published a small pamphlet with the challenging title, "What Is Being Taught in the Public Schools? HUMANISM!" In it he wrote:

> "Few have read or understood the *Humanist Manifesto*, as also was the case with Adolph Hitler's *Mein Kampf*. How tragic for mankind that complacency, and failure to act, brought millions to the gas chambers, millions more to the yoke of Communist slavery and to genocide, and further millions to the bankruptcy of Humanism. The Nazis, Communists and Humanists told the world their intentions and unheeding generations perished.
>
> "Suffice it to say that John Dewey and others of the same mind lost no time in seizing the public school classrooms (and most institutions of higher learning) as pulpits for instilling the Humanistic doctrine. Today, the list of Humanist educrats, teachers, and preachers, even at the hierarchy, would fill many pages."

Constitutional Issue

All of the above comments raise serious questions as to the constitutionality of government funding, at the expense of taxpayers at large, of a school system that is based on a religion as clearly enunciated not only in the *Humanist Manifesto* itself, but also in interpretations by *Webster's Dictionary,* and by the Supreme Court in the *Torcaso v. Watkins* case.

Since the philosophy contained in the *Humanist Manifesto,* per John Dewey, is the "religion" of our public school system, it becomes evident that government support of that religion, via coercive taxes, violates the First Amendment admonition that "Congress shall make no law respecting an establishment of religion."

In addition, when U.S. governments allocate tax funds to a school system that advances the religion of Humanism, but denies such funds to school systems that advance other religions, such as Christianity and Judaism, U.S. governments are also guilty of violating the "equal protection" clause of the Fourteenth Amendment.

In sum, the government-run public school system functions as a de facto enabler of religious Humanism, which, in turn, functions as an adversary against traditional religions. This fact raises serious constitutional questions as to the propriety of government allocation of tax funds to a religious system that is a giant adversary against traditional God-fearing religions, which are supposed to be protected under the First Amendment.

Suffice it to say here that the *Humanist Manifesto*, and the prominent role that John Dewey played in drafting that document, and the extent to which he injected these philosophies into our public school system—as evidenced by his high standing in the National Education Association—raises serious questions that can no longer be swept under the amoral carpet of Humanism.

We shall address these questions in subsequent chapters.

6

The First Amendment of the U.S. Constitution

Radical Change Is Necessary

Having determined that our public education system is adrift in a moral vacuum, and that it is beyond redemption in its present form, it becomes obvious that a radical change is mandatory. The change must be so radical, indeed, that the public school establishment, with the help of the American Civil Liberties Union (ACLU), People for the American Way (PAW), Americans United for Separation of Church and State, and other anti–God-fearing religious groups, will necessarily marshal all their forces to oppose it . . . without credibility.

It is crucial, therefore, to the future of our nation for all who recognize the bankruptcy of our present education system to join forces, with an open mind, to construct an educational system based on moral principles, responsibility, freedom, and the U.S. Constitution.

That may be difficult, or impossible, if we insist on going along with certain myths and false impressions that have taken center stage in the propaganda mills of antireligion groups, the media, and in the narrow minds of many who are the indoctrinated products of the Marx/Dewey public school monopoly.

The first requisite in our search for solutions is that we keep an open mind . . . that we are willing to question, indeed reject, prevailing "wisdom," so that we can see beyond its façade. Unless we do, we will never set foot on the right road.

The Founding of America

Along with many other strict constitutionalists (like Robert Bork), I believe the U.S. Constitution deserves the classification of "sacred" rather than a "living" document subject to the whims of special-interest groups. In our search for solutions, let's keep in mind the visions of the Founding Fathers who drafted the sacred documents on which this nation is founded. When the Declaration of Independence and the U.S. Constitution were drafted, there was no such thing as a public school system. The notion that the federal government would be involved in a public education system was the farthest thing from the minds of those who drafted our Constitution.

Most elementary and secondary schools were small, and most were affiliated with religious bodies, including churches. There was no nationwide, or even statewide, public education system funded by a general tax. Moreover, most political leaders had strong religious convictions. The United States of America was founded on Judeo-Christian beliefs and principles. There were a variety of religious denominations, but they all shared a reverence for an Almighty God, a Divine Providence and, as Thomas Jefferson wrote in the Declaration of Independence, a reliance on our "Creator."

West's Encyclopedia of American Law

This background information is from *West's Encyclopedia of American Law*, volume 8, West Group, 1998, pages 304–306. Copyright © 1998 by WEST GROUP. Reprinted by permission of The Gale Group.

" . . . In the early nineteenth century, the vast majority of Americans were Protestant, and Protestant-based religious exercises were common in public schools. . . . Until 1962 when the U.S. Supreme Court began to directly address some of these issues, most states upheld the constitutionality of prayer and Bible reading in the public schools.

"In the 1962 case of *Engels v. Vitale*, . . . the Supreme Court struck down as unconstitutional a prayer that was a recommended part of the public school curriculum in the State of New York. The prayer had been approved by Protestant, Catholic, and Jewish leaders. . . . Although the prayer was non-denominational and student participation in it was strictly voluntary, it was struck down as violative of the Establishment Clause.

"Because the Establishment Clause calls for government neutrality in matters involving religion, the government need not be hostile or unfriendly toward religions because such an approach would favor those who do not believe in religion over those who do. [And that would trample on the 'equal protection' clause of the Fourteenth Amendment, as well as the 'free exercise' clause.] In addition, if the government denies religious speakers the ability to speak, or punishes them for their speech, it violates the First Amendment's right to FREEDOM OF SPEECH. The Supreme Court held in 1981 that it was unconstitutional for a state university to prohibit a religious group from using its facilities when the facilities were open for use by organizations of all other kinds (*Widmar v. Vincent*). . . . The principles established in *Widmar* were unanimously reaffirmed . . . in *Lamb's Chapel v. Center Moriches Union Free School District.* . . . In 1995 the Supreme Court held that a state university violates the Free Speech Clause when it refuses to pay for a religious organization's publication under a program in which it pays for other student organization publications *(Rosenberger v. Rector and Visitors of the Univ. of Virginia).* . . .

Creating a Better Education System

Any attempt to create an education system based on moral values as well as academics must involve some measure of competition, or "choice," that would allow parents to send their children to schools of their own free choosing, including private secular and religiously oriented (parochial) schools.

That, of course, is when the public school establishment, and antireligion organizations like the ACLU and PAW, and Barry Lynn, Executive Director of Americans United for Separation of Church and State, go into a virtual tizzy screaming that such "freedom" would violate the "wall of separation between church and state," which, they say, is embodied in the First Amendment of the U.S. Constitution.

However, there is no such statement anywhere in the Constitution. No less an authority than Chief Justice William Rehnquist has repeatedly said so. Here is what the First Amendment of the U.S. Constitution *does* say on this subject:

The First Amendment

☆ "Congress shall make no law respecting an establishment of religion, or prohibiting the free exercise thereof; or abridging the freedom of speech, or of the press; or the right of people peaceably to assemble, and to petition the Government for a redress of grievances."

Obviously, the phrase "wall of separation between church and state" does not appear in the First Amendment or any other part of the Constitution.

Freedom of Speech and Freedom of Religion

Some, like former President Jimmy Carter, have gone so far as to say "religion should stay out of politics." But such views are contrary to the fact that the First Amendment does endorse the "free exercise of religion," as well as "freedom of speech" and "to petition the Government."

☆ These freedoms are extended to all citizens without qualification or exceptions. Nowhere does the First Amendment say or imply that these freedoms are granted "except on public property, or in politics, or in schools." The Constitution contains no restriction of any kind on the free exercise of religion, freedom of speech, or the right to petition the government.

To deny religiously oriented people the right to be involved in politics would not only be a violation of the free exercise clause, it would also violate the free speech clause, which is contained in the same sentence as the free exercise clause. Any denial of the right of religious people to express their views in the political arena or on public property would relegate them to second-class citizens and would also violate the equal protection clause of the Fourteenth Amendment.

For further clarification let's go back again to the *Encyclopedia of Religion in American Politics* (1999, page 108):

"The U.S. Supreme Court has developed the principle that government constraints on freedom of expression based on the content of the speech itself are unconstitutional barring some 'compelling' state interest in regulating the speech. In *Widmar v. Vincent* (1981), the Supreme Court applied this general doctrine to a situation with implications for religious liberty. The Court ruled that once a state university makes its facilities available for use by student groups, it may not forbid a religious student group access to those facilities without compelling reason. The Court argued that the university in this case, which made its decision as part of a general policy prohibiting use of facilities 'for purposes of religious worship or religious teaching,' was burdening particular forms of expression in violation of the First Amendment right to free speech.

"The Court's basic reasoning in *Widmar* has been influential in subsequent rules on religious freedom. The issue in *Lamb's Chapel v. Center Moriches Union Free School District* (1993), for example, was a public school board's refusal to grant a church equal access to school property to show a film on family issues. The Court held that the district, which had refused only religious treatments of such topics, had not designed a content-neutral policy toward all types of expression. Even public funding of various groups must maintain neutrality. In *Rosenberger v. Rector and Visitors of the University of Virginia* (1995), the Court invalidated the University of Virginia's policy of withholding certain funds for religious student groups (mainly printing costs for a group's publication). The Court argued that the university could not choose which groups to fund solely on the basis of the views expressed by those groups.

"As a matter of constitutional jurisprudence, the free speech approach to religious liberty is in its infancy. Yet we might expect greater reliance on the approach if the Court continues to maintain its equal access doctrine."

The Myth of Separation of Church and State

Antireligion forces routinely contend that Thomas Jefferson was quoting the Constitution when he used the phrase "separation of church and state." Of course, as we have seen in the above exact phraseology of the First Amendment, there is no such phrase in that Amendment. Instead, it has been lifted, out of context, from a letter by President Thomas Jefferson, in 1802, in response to an inquiry from the Danbury Baptist Association.

There was no implication in his statement that religion should stay out of politics, or that there is a wall that cannot be scaled by religion.

- ☆ To the contrary, that "wall" was built into our Constitution to keep *government* out of religious matters, not to constrain religiously oriented people.
- ☆ That is why the free exercise clause was injected into the First Amendment: to guarantee the right of every citizen to practice their religion, including the right to reflect it in political matters. That right is further guaranteed in the free speech clause, which is contained in the same sentence as the establishment and free exercise clauses.
- ☆ Thus, the establishment clause cannot be interpreted in isolation. It must always be weighed in conjunction with the free exercise and free speech clauses.

Moreover, anything that Jefferson or anyone else may have said before or after the Constitution and the First Amendment were ratified is irrelevant. Unless a statement specifically appears in the Constitution it has no legal standing. The

Constitution is a binding contract with "We, the People," as stipulated in the Preamble.

As such, it is similar to a contract between the owner of an apartment complex and one of its renters. If the contract does not say that the apartment owner will pay for the cost of utilities, no amount of argument by a renter that a salesman said so will stand up in court. The contract is what it says in the contract. The Constitution is what it says in the Constitution, notwithstanding any comments by anyone before or after the Constitution was ratified.

George Washington Speaks

As an indication of the mood of our Founding Fathers, instead of listening to the misguided comments of Jimmy Carter, it would serve a more useful purpose to heed the words of the father of our country, George Washington. He was not only the leader of the Revolutionary Forces to free our people from the tyrannical rule of King George, he was also president of the Continental Congress, chairman of the meeting of fifty-five men in Philadelphia when the Constitution was drafted, and the first president of the newly formed United States of America. Here is what he said in his farewell address:

- ☆ "Of all the dispositions and habits which lead to political prosperity, religion and morality are indispensable supports. In vain would that man labor to subvert these great pillars of human happiness, these firmest props of the duties of men and citizens. The mere politician, equally with the pious man, ought to respect and cherish them."
- ☆ "Let it simply be asked, Where is the security for property, for reputation, for life, if the sense of religious obligation desert the oaths which are the instruments of investigation in courts of justice?"

☆ "And, let us with caution indulge the supposition that morality can be maintained without religion."

What Others Had to Say

John Adams put it this way: "We have no government armed with power capable of contending with human passion unbridled by morality and religion. Our Constitution was made only for a moral and religious people. It is wholly inadequate to the government of any other."

Thomas Jefferson asked this question: "Can the liberties of a nation be secure when we remove their only firm basis, a conviction in the minds of the people that these liberties are the gift of God?"

James Madison, the primary author of the First Amendment, expressed clear and strong views on the subject of religious establishment and liberty in his "Memorial and Remonstrance Against Religious Assessments" (1785). He wrote: "We maintain, therefore, that in matters of Religion, no man's right is abridged by the institution of Civil Society, and that Religion is wholly exempt from its cognizance . . . (and) if Religion be exempt from the authority of the Society at large, still less can it be subject to that of the Legislative Body."

Finally, in their classic book, *The Lessons of History*, Will and Ariel Durant asked: "Does history warrant the conclusion that religion is necessary to morality . . . that a natural ethic is too weak to withstand the savagery that lurks under civilization and emerges in our dreams, crimes and wars?" Their answer was, "There is no significant example in history of society successfully maintaining moral life without the aid of religion."

With that preface let us now examine the words and intent of the First Amendment.

The Establishment Clause

Antireligious forces rest virtually all their contentions on the establishment clause with seldom any reference to the free exercise and free speech clauses. But the establishment clause cannot and should not be interpreted separately from the free exercise and free speech clauses that are contained in the same sentence.

The establishment clause reads as follows: "Congress shall make no law respecting an establishment of religion."

It is commonly, and correctly, interpreted that Congress should not bestow on any *particular* religion its special approval, in a way that would give it the status of a "state-sanctioned" religion with preferential status, as was the case in England.

The Free Exercise Clause

For that reason, the clause "prohibit the free exercise thereof" is especially significant. Clearly, it was the intent of the Framers that neither Congress (and by extension any arm of government) should prohibit the "free exercise" of religion. Thus, the free exercise clause is dominant. The establishment clause becomes subservient to the free exercise clause.

Obviously, if "free exercise" of religion is the law of the land, Congress (and no other government body) could "establish" a state religion as in England, because that would be in conflict with the free exercise clause. It would be an oxymoron. Thus, the establishment clause is secondary to the free exercise clause. The establishment clause simply reinforces the free exercise clause, which remains dominant.

Interpreting the Establishment Clause

The establishment clause needs further clarification. The term "respecting" means "with respect to" or "with regard to."

Thus, the clause would read: "Congress shall make no law with regard to (or with respect to) an establishment of religion."

> ☆ When viewed in that manner, the logical interpretation is that government should make no law or edict involving religion, either in favor of or against religion or an existing religious establishment. In other words, government should remain neutral in all matters of religion. As cited earlier herein, the Supreme Court has consistently ruled that government must remain neutral in matters of religion.

In that context it would be wrong for, let us say, a public school principal to deny the use of school facilities to a Bible study group of students during after-class hours. That would constitute a "law with regard to an establishment of religion," which is forbidden under the First Amendment, especially if school facilities are used by other groups. In this latter case, denial of facilities to a Bible study group, while other groups are granted such rights, would also violate the equal protection clause of the Fourteenth Amendment.

When taken in context with the free exercise clause, this is a matter of considerable significance in view of an increasing tendency among government bodies and their administrators, such as teachers and school principals, to take action *against* religion and its free exercise. In making such edicts they violate the establishment clause, which says they "shall make no law with regard to an establishment of religion."

More Examples

Examples include occasions when a school administrator reprimands a student for saying a prayer during graduation ceremonies or prior to a high school football game, or reprimands a student for referring to God in an oral composition, or refuses to allow the Boy Scouts to meet on school property on a premise that the Boy Scouts require its members to profess belief in God. Such dictates constitute "a law with respect to an establishment of religion," and that is contrary to the letter and spirit of the establishment clause as well as the free exercise clause!

In October 1998, the Denver Zoning Administration ordered Diane Reiter and her husband, David, to cease and desist from hosting a monthly Bible study in their home for nine to fifteen people. The Reiter's legal appeal was denied by the Zoning Board, which informed the Reiters that "If they were having a weekly 'book club' meeting in their home rather than a 'prayer meeting' there would likely be no problem." Such arbitrary and exclusionary actions violate the First Amendment.

In the aftermath of the massacre at Columbine High School in Littleton, Colorado, several members of the community planned a memorial on school grounds in honor of the victims. But they soon ran into opposition from others who said that memorial would be a violation of "separation of church and state." When a local carpenter erected several crosses as memorials to the victims, it prompted more objections that they were "religious." When he proposed to erect them in a nearby park, the park manager said, "I know there are some people who would like to see a religious memorial, but if it is to be erected in the park, we can't let you do it by law. The Constitution won't permit it!" Of course, the Constitution says nothing like what the manager said, or what he may have been told by his superiors.

New Jersey Court v. Boy Scouts of America

From these perspectives, the New Jersey Supreme Court's "edict" that the Boy Scouts of America cannot refuse to allow an admitted homosexual to serve as a Scout leader is clearly a violation of the U.S. Constitution. The Boy Scouts, for nearly one hundred years, has been a religiously oriented organization, as witnessed by the fact that its members must profess a belief in God and biblical teachings. Thus, the Boy Scouts of America is "an establishment based on religious principles." The First Amendment mandates that Congress (and by extension, no branch of government) can make a law, or an edict, respecting (which is to say, with regard to) an "establishment" of religion.

Therefore, by merely entertaining the ACLU lawsuit, in behalf of the homosexual against the Boy Scouts, the New Jersey Supreme Court put itself in an untenable position. Whether the Court ruled in favor of or against the Boy Scouts, it would be "making a law respecting an establishment of religion" in violation of the First Amendment. Either way it ruled, it would be violating the First Amendment, which says, "shall make no law with regard to (or with respect to) an establishment of religion." Simultaneously, the Court's decision against the Boy Scouts violated the free exercise clause.

Government Must Remain Neutral

The important point to keep in mind in these observations is that the establishment and the free exercise clauses prohibit any government agency from making *any* edict *for* or *against* religion.

> ☆ In other words, government should stay out of religious matters . . . either for or against! Government must not take any action that would interfere with the free exercise of religion.

More Interpretations of the Establishment Clause

The First Amendment says, "Congress shall make no law respecting an establishment of religion." In that context the word "establishment" is a noun. It has the same significance as to say "no law respecting an establishment of groceries, or shoe repair." As a noun, the word "establishment" relates to an *existing* entity or one that may be formed in the future. The word "an" qualifies that noun by giving it the meaning of "any" existing or future establishment of. . . .

Now let us rephrase the clause to read: "Congress shall make no law respecting *the* establishment of religion." We have simply changed the small word "an" to "the." The word "establishment" becomes like a verb . . . meaning an *action* that would "establish a religion," such as a new religion in which government played a part. That, of course, would be a clear prohibition against a state religion such as prevailed in England. But, that is not what the First Amendment says. In nearly all legal cases establishment has been interpreted as an action by government, i.e., to establish a religion. Yet the phrase is couched as a noun.

Instead, it says, "make no law respecting (with regards to) an establishment of religion," which is to infer that the restriction pertains to any infringement on an *existing* religious institution, or "establishment," or any that may be formed in the future.

In that context, the establishment clause says, in effect, that Congress (and by extension any other branch of government) may not make any law or pass any edict with regard to *any* religion or any religious organization that may currently exist or that may be formed in the future. It simply means, as has already been stated, government should make no law or edict that has anything to do with religion, or a religious institution, unless there are "compelling" reasons to do so.

> ✮ In other words, government should stay out of the free exercise of religion . . . to be neither for or against any religion or any religious establishment.

Purpose of the First Amendment

It is vitally important to understand that the primary purpose of the First Amendment was to guarantee freedom OF religion, not FROM religion! The emphasis is on the positive aspects of all religious pursuits, not on the negative. The words "of" and "from" may be small, and there may be a tendency to disregard such a small difference, but that difference is of overwhelming significance.

Nothing in the First Amendment even remotely suggests that any phase of our political and social order should be free "from" religion, or the moral principles embodied in nearly all religious denominations, including the free speech right to inject religious beliefs and moral principles in the political arena . . . and on public property.

No responsible member of the Christian Coalition or any other religious organization has suggested that anyone be denied the right to pursue their own chosen faith, and they certainly do not seek to establish a state religion.

Instead, they attempt to inject into the political debate basic moral principles that have stood the test of time since Moses came down from the mountain with a tablet containing the Ten Commandments, which have been endorsed in varying ways by nearly all religions and by the majority of morally responsible people. To say these principles should not be involved in the political process is antireligion bigotry of the highest order and a flat-out disregard for the First Amendment.

This, of course, places a different interpretation on the First Amendment as compared with those who view the First Amendment only as a measure to prevent government from being "for" a religion.

> ☆ It is vitally important for us to acknowledge that the First Amendment prohibits any branch of government from acting *against* religion in any manner! Instead,

government must protect the right of every citizen to freely exercise his or her religion.

☆ The First Amendment is a declaration of what government can *not* do. It was never intended to "separate" church from state, but to prohibit the state from *any* infringement on the free exercise of religion. The First Amendment does not, nor was it intended to, construct a wall that could not be scaled by religious pursuit, thought, or expression.

Thus, contrary to those who decry the involvement of religiously oriented people, like Jerry Falwell, Pat Robertson, Ralph Reed, and the Christian Coalition, in the political and election process, the First Amendment guarantees their right to do so just like any other citizen.

It is disturbing, therefore, that influential members of the press, who fervently argue in behalf of "free speech and a free press"—so as to serve their own special interests—would deny those rights to people of religious persuasion, even to the extent of calling them "extremists, right-wingers, bigots, etc."

From these perspectives the decision by the New Jersey Supreme Court that the Boy Scouts must allow an admitted homosexual to function as a Scout leader must be viewed as an infringement on the free exercise rights of the Boy Scouts, whose religious beliefs hold that there is a God and that homosexuality is a sin. In that decision, the New Jersey Supreme Court acted in a discriminatory manner against the Boy Scouts in violation of both the establishment and free exercise clauses. Ironically, it also violated its own state law that banned discrimination.

Fortunately, on June 28, 2000, in *Boy Scouts of America v. Dale*, the U.S. Supreme Court, by a 5-to-4 majority vote, overturned the New Jersey Court's ruling. In behalf of the majority Chief Justice William H. Rehnquist wrote to uphold the Boy Scouts' "First Amendment expressive association right. It is not the role of the courts to reject a group's expressed values because they disagree with those values. The Boy Scouts assert that it teaches that homosexual conduct is not morally straight, and that it does not want to promote homosexual conduct as a legitimate form of behavior. We accept the Boy Scouts' assertion." Justices Scalia, Thomas, Kennedy, and O'Connor concurred.

The Meaning of the Free Exercise Clause

We should also weigh the significance of the clause, "or prohibit the free exercise thereof." What do these words mean?

Webster's Dictionary defines "prohibit" as "denying, restraining, or interfering with, certain activities." Thus, it is proper to interpret the clause as follows: "Neither Congress, or any other arm of government, should deny, restrain, or interfere with the free exercise of religion."

Webster's also defines "free" as "without interference or hindrance, unrestrained, unrestricted, without cost or penalty, etc." Thus, *anything* that government may do to interfere with, restrain, restrict, hamper, or penalize the "free" exercise of religion is contrary to what that clause says and intends.

And so, this clause might now read as follows: ". . . nor interfere with the free, unrestrained, unrestricted exercise of religion, without cost or penalty of any kind." That is what the free exercise clause really says and intends. In other words, to put it bluntly, government should not interfere with the ability of people to freely exercise their religion . . . in any way, period!

The Meaning of "Exercise"

We cannot leave this clause without also determining the significance of the word "exercise." The framers did not simply say "or prohibiting freedom of religion." They deliberately inserted the word "exercise" to underscore the right of every American to "exercise" their religious beliefs, and to do it in a tangible manner "free" of government intervention or restriction.

This goes beyond simply saying "freedom *of* religion," as though that is something you keep to yourself, within your mind or heart.

No, indeed. Every person is granted the right to "exercise" it . . . to apply it . . . to expand it . . . to act on it . . . to practice it in all its forms, including sending their children to a church or school, that honors their religious beliefs. It is not just an abstract thing that may take place at bedside in the privacy of a home, or something just between a human being and God.

No, indeed, you have a right to exercise it wherever and whenever you please, including the perpetuation of that religion in your children, without restraint or restriction.

The Court Speaks Again

In *Cantwell v. State of Connecticut* (1940), the Supreme Court further distinguished between the free exercise of religion as *belief* and the free exercise of religion as *action*. The Court held that "the Amendment embraces two concepts—freedom to believe and freedom to act."

Thus the freedom to "act" in the "exercise" of religion must not be abridged, so long as it does not violate laws designed to protect society at large. If such "exercise" does not violate that premise, the state must not interfere with the "free exercise" of religion.

The next few chapters will reveal how government *does* interfere with the free exercise of religion and what must be done to stop the State from violating the First Amendment.

7

Putting God Back in the Public Square

With thanks and appreciation to Hillsdale College, in Hillsdale, Michigan, and Judge Roy S. Moore, this chapter is a digest of Judge Moore's remarks in the summer 1999 issue of the *Cumberland Law Review*, as reproduced in the August 1999 issue of *Imprimis*, a monthly publication of Hillsdale College.

Hillsdale College holds the unique distinction of being one of only two private colleges that refuses to accept funding from any government agency so that it may remain free from any government interference in its curricula and administration.

Since 1992, Roy S. Moore has been a circuit judge for the 16th Judicial District in Etowah County, Alabama. A former deputy district attorney, he is also a Vietnam veteran who served as a captain, a company commander, and a battalion staff officer in the military police corps. He graduated from the U.S. Military Academy at West Point in 1969 and the University of Alabama School of Law in 1977.

For his achievements in the community and on the bench, Judge Moore has received awards from numerous national organizations, including the Center for Christian Statesmanship, the Family Research Council, and The American Family Association. Judge Moore's seven-year battle to preserve religious freedom of expression in the courtroom and in the public arena has earned him national media attention.

Twice in recent years Judge Moore has been sued for displaying the Ten Commandments in his courtroom. But he has remained steadfast in his right to do so. On November 7, 2000, Alabama voters showed their respect by elevating him to Chief Justice of the State Supreme Court. Here then with his permission are his remarks as they appeared in *Imprimis*.

"In his first official act, President George Washington did something that would be unthinkable today. He prayed in public during his inaugural address!

> Specifically, he made fervent supplications to that Almighty Being who rules over the universe, who presides in the councils of nations, and whose providential aids can supply every human defect, that His benediction may consecrate to the liberties and happiness of the people of the United States a Government instituted by themselves for these essential purposes . . . No people can be bound to acknowledge and adore the Invisible Hand which conducts the affairs of men more than the people of the United States. Every step by which they have advanced to the character of an independent nation seems to

have been distinguished by some token of providential agency.'

"If that were not enough, Washington added, 'We ought to be no less persuaded that the propitious smiles of Heaven can never be expected on a nation that disregards the eternal rules of order and right which Heaven itself has ordained.'

"Two hundred years later, few government officials are bold enough to make earnest professions of faith. It seems that politicians can do just about anything in public but pray, unless it is obligatory (during, say, an annual prayer breakfast at the White House). They can survive scandal and immoral conduct, but they suffer ostracism and worse once they are labeled members of the 'Religious Right.'

"Even the American justice system, which is firmly rooted in the Judeo-Christian tradition, has developed a bias against public worship and the public acknowledgment of God that ought to give the most militant atheist cause for concern. If judges can deny Christians and Jews the right to express their beliefs in the public square, they can surely deny secular humanists (devout believers of a different sort [a la John Dewey]) the same right.

"In California, creches and crosses have been removed from downtown Christmas and Easter displays.

"In Kansas, city hall monuments featuring religious symbols have been torn down.

"In Rhode Island, high school graduation invocations and benedictions have been banned.

"In Alabama, students have been prohibited by federal court order from praying, from distributing religious materials, and from even discussing anything of a devotional or inspirational nature with their classmates and teachers.

"And in Ohio, an appellate court . . . overturned the sentence of a man convicted of raping an eight-year-old child ten times. Why? Because the judge who pronounced the sentence quoted from the 18th chapter of Matthew: 'But whoso shall offend one of these little ones which believe in me, it were better for him that a millstone were hanged about his neck, and that he were drowned in the depth of the sea.'

"In the courtroom in which I preside, the public display of the Ten Commandments and voluntary clergy-led prayer prior to jury organizational sessions have sparked not only a national controversy but also an epic legal battle. In 1995, I was sued in federal court by the ACLU and the Alabama Freethought Association. Just prior to that case being dismissed for lack of standing (the ACLU and Alabama Freethought Association failed to show that they had been or were about to be injured), a separate lawsuit was filed in Alabama state court requesting a ruling on whether the First Amendment to the United States Constitution prohibits the display of the Ten Commandments and voluntary prayer in the courtroom. A state circuit court judge presiding in Montgomery County, Alabama, held that the practices in Etowah County were unconstitutional under the First Amendment's 'Establishment Clause,' which reads, 'Congress shall make no law respecting an establishment of religion. . . .' It would appear that the circuit court judge and others were not impressed when the members of the U.S. House of Representatives and the U.S. Senate passed a resolution stating that

> (1) the Ten Commandments are a declaration of fundamental principles that are the cornerstones of a fair and just society; and

> (2) the public display, including display in government offices and courthouses, of the Ten Commandments should be permitted.

"The state circuit court's ruling was appealed to the Alabama Supreme Court and, appropriately, was set aside by the Alabama Supreme Court in 1998. Nevertheless, federal constitutional issues regarding public worship and the public acknowledgment of God remain unresolved.

"Church and State

"In a 1997 law review article, Brian T. Collidge expressed the opinion of many in the legal profession when he claimed that the mere display of the Ten Commandments in the courtroom is a 'dangerous' practice. Although Collidge concedes that the Commandments reflect universal teachings that are beneficial to a civil society, they make explicit references to God, and, in his view, this is an unconstitutional breach of the 'wall of separation between church and state.'

"This now famous 'wall of separation' phrase does not appear in the Constitution, the Declaration of Independence, the Articles of Confederation, or any other official

American document, yet millions of Americans have been led to believe that it does and that, in the words found in a 1947 Supreme Court decision, '[t]he wall must be kept high and impregnable.'

"The phrase is actually mentioned for the first time in a letter President Thomas Jefferson wrote in 1802 in reply to an inquiry from the Danbury Baptist Association. Jefferson said,

> 'Believing with you that religion is a matter which lies solely between man and his God; that he owes account to none other for his faith or his worship; that the legislative powers of government reach actions only, and not opinions, I contemplate with sovereign reverence that act of the whole American people which declared that their legislature should make no law respecting an establishment of religion, or prohibiting the free exercise thereof, thus building a wall of separation between church and state.'

"But did Jefferson mean that the government should in no way support religion? To find the answer we must go back more than one hundred years before he wrote to the Danbury Baptist Association. Jefferson was strongly influenced by John Locke, a well-known English philosopher, who published 'A Letter Concerning Toleration' in 1689 in which he clearly defined the proper church-state relationship. Locke stated that '[t]he magistrate has no power to enforce by law, either in his own Church, or much less in another, the use of any rites or forms of worship by the force of his laws.'

"Herein lies the true meaning of separation between church and state as the concept was understood by Jefferson and the other founding fathers: Government may never dictate one's form of worship or articles of faith. Not all public worship of God must be halted; on the contrary, freedom to engage in such worship was the very reason for creating a doctrine of separation between church and state.

"Two days after he wrote to the Danbury Baptist Association, Jefferson attended a church service conducted by John Leland, a prominent Baptist minister, in the halls of the House of Representatives. Throughout his presidency, he attended similar services, which were often held in the north wing of the Capitol. From 1807 to 1857 church services were held in a variety of government buildings where Congress, the Supreme Court, the War Office, and the Treasury were headquartered.

"Obviously, neither Jefferson nor any other officials in the early Republic understood separation between church and state to mean that the federal government was precluded from recognizing the necessity of public worship or from permitting active support of opportunities for such worship. Indeed, they plainly recognized that the duty of civil government was to encourage public professions of faith. Perhaps this is why John Jay, the first Chief Justice of the Supreme Court, specifically authorized the opening of jury sessions over which he presided with voluntary prayer led by local clergy of the Christian faith.

"Many believe that James Madison, as chief architect of the Constitution and the Bill of Rights, led the fight to keep religion out of politics. In truth, he was more interested in protecting religion from politics. In 1785, two years before the Constitutional Convention, he wrote a *Memorial and Remonstrance* opposing a Virginia bill to establish a provision for teachers of the Christian religion. He stated that . . . 'religion, or the duty which we owe to our Creator, and the manner of discharging it,' was a right and a duty 'precedent both in order of time and degree of obligation, to the claims of a civil society. Before any man can be considered as a member of civil society, he must be considered as a subject of the Governor of the Universe.'

"Madison championed the First Amendment's Establishment Clause with one overriding purpose: to keep one sect from gaining an advantage over another through political patronage. This is a far cry from denying public worship or the public acknowledgment of God. Madison also made sure that the Establishment Clause was followed by the 'Free Exercise Clause,' so that the First Amendment would read, in relevant part, 'Congress shall make no law respecting an establishment of religion, *or prohibiting the free exercise thereof. . . .*'

"Both Jefferson and Madison would have agreed with United States Supreme Court Justice Joseph Story's definitive *Commentaries on the Constitution of the United States* (1833) in which he posed the question of whether any free government could endure if it failed to provide for public worship. They would have concluded, as did Justice Story, that it could not. Justice Story explained that:

> '[t]he promulgation of the great doctrines of religion, the being, and attributes, and providence of one Almighty God, the responsibility to him for all our actions, founded on moral freedom and accountability; a future state of rewards and punishments; the cultivation of all the personal, social and benevolent virtues; these never can be a matter of indifference in any well ordered community. It is, indeed, difficult to conceive, how any civilized society can well exist without them.'

"Historical Precedent

"When the federal legislature met in 1789, one of its first actions was to appoint chaplains in both houses of Congress. (Congress still recognizes God by appointing and paying chaplains who open each session with a prayer—even the recent session devoted to the impeachment proceedings against President Clinton.)

"On the very day that Congress approved the wording of the First Amendment, its members resolved to request of President Washington a day of public thanksgiving and prayer for the peaceful manner in which the Constitution was formed.

"A month earlier, Congress passed the Northwest Ordinance, one of the most important documents in our history. Article III of the Ordinance declared, 'Religion, morality, and knowledge, being necessary to good government and the happiness of mankind, schools and the means of education shall forever be encouraged.'

"Every president of the United States (with only one possible exception) has been administered the oath of office with his hand on the Bible, ending with the words 'so help me God.'

"The Supreme Court begins every proceeding with the ringing proclamation, 'God save the United States and this Honorable Court.'

"Throughout our history, the executive and legislative branches have decreed national days of fasting and prayer.

"Public offices and public schools close in observance of religious holidays.

"United States currency bears our national motto, 'In God We Trust.'

"Also by law, the Pledge of Allegiance to the Flag affirms that we are 'one nation under God.' Congress would not even allow a comma to be placed after the word 'nation' in order to reflect the basic idea that ours is a 'nation founded on a belief in God.'

"It is ludicrous and illogical to believe that it is constitutionally permissible for all three branches of the federal government to acknowledge God openly and publicly on a regular basis, and yet at the same time accept the notion that the federal government can strictly prohibit the states from doing the very same thing. Have we become so ignorant of our nation's history that we have forgotten the reason for the adoption of the Bill of Rights? It was meant to restrict the federal government's power over the states, not to restrict the states from doing what the federal government can do.

"It is no wonder that our present Supreme Court Chief Justice William Rehnquist observed in a 1985 dissenting opinion that 'the wall of separation between church and state is a metaphor based upon bad history, a metaphor which has proved useless as a guide to judging. It should be frankly and explicitly abandoned.'

"Rehnquist added that 'the greatest injury of the "wall" notion is its mischievous diversion of judges from the actual intention of the drafters of the Bill of Rights.' He is right. The doctrine of separation between church and state has been abused, twisted, and taken out of context in recent court decisions in order to prevent the public worship and acknowledgment of God.

"False Neutrality

"The Pharisees demanded of Jesus, 'Is it lawful to give tribute unto Caesar, or not?' He asked them to produce a coin and tell him whose image was inscribed on its face. When they replied, 'Caesar's,' Jesus gave his answer: 'Render therefore unto Caesar the things that are Caesar's, and unto God the things that are God's.'

"We have to render an awful lot to Caesar these days, but we do not and should not surrender our freedom of conscience. The state can't tell us how we ought to think or what we ought to believe. As Jefferson testified, 'Almighty God hath created the mind free.'

"But in the latter half of the 20th century the state is trying to take by force the unalienable rights freely given to us by God, declared in the Declaration of Independence to be 'self evident.' Caesar is trying to tell us when, where, and how we can profess our faith.

"In 1962 the Supreme Court outlawed a simple, 22-word, nondenominational prayer devised by the New York Board of Regents and used in the New York public schools: 'Almighty God, we acknowledge our dependence upon thee, and we beg thy blessings upon us, our parents, our teachers, and our country.'

"A year later the Court issued another ruling declaring that reading the Bible and reciting the Lord's Prayer in Pennsylvania and Maryland public schools [were] unconstitutional, thus outlawing 'without the citation of a single case' practices that had existed in American schools for over 170 years. Writing for the majority, Justice Tom C. Clark asserted, 'In the relationship between man and religion, the state is firmly committed to a position of neutrality.' Justice Potter Stewart pointed out in his lone dissent that this was false neutrality indeed, designed to stifle public professions of faith. Justice Stewart also noted, 'We err in the first place if we do not recognize, as a matter of history and matter of the imperatives of our free society, that religion and government must necessarily interact in countless ways.'

"Both decisions represented a major turning point in our history. Judges were no longer interested in the 'original intent' of the founders or in legal precedents (which they unapologetically and arrogantly failed to cite). They were eager to embrace the new doctrine of 'judicial activism,' which would allow them the opportunity to use their power to reshape society according to the attitudes and whims of the changing times.

"Since the 1960s judicial activists have made a concerted effort to banish God from the public square. They have done this by deliberately destroying the distinction between 'religion' and 'religious activity.' These terms may sound similar, but in fact they are very different. Religious activities may include many actions that would not themselves constitute religion. For example, prayer and Bible reading might be characterized as religious activities, but they do not constitute religion, and they are not limited to any specific sect or even to religious people. One may read the New Testament to gain wisdom, and school students may pray before a big exam. Neither activity was intended to be, is, or should be, proscribed by the First Amendment, even if practiced in public.

"Sadly, however, it seems that the judicial activists are winning the war. Consider the 1997 case in Dekalb

County, Alabama. There, a federal district court determined that a student's brief prayer during a high school graduation ceremony was a violation of the First Amendment because it allegedly coerced unwilling citizens to participate in religious activity. We have evidently forgotten that nothing in the Constitution guarantees that an individual won't have to see and hear things that are disagreeable or offensive to him. We have also failed to realize that peer pressure and public opinion are not the types of coercion against which the framers were seeking to safeguard.

"No student should ever be forced by law to participate in prayer or in other religious activity. But to outlaw the public acknowledgment of God simply because another student might have to witness it is as illogical as abandoning a school mascot or motto because it might not be every student's favorite or because some might not believe in 'school spirit.'

"In this context, Justice Joseph Story is again worth quoting. He said: '[T]he duty of supporting religion, and especially the Christian religion, is very different from the right to force the consciences of other men, or to punish them for worshipping God in the manner which they believe their accountability to him requires.' Even more to the point, one of the most famous Supreme Court justices, William O. Douglas, once wrote that forbidding public worship discriminates in favor of 'those who believe in no religion over those who do believe.'

"*Disastrous Consequences*

"October 1997—Pearl, Mississippi; December 1997—Paducah, Kentucky; March 1998—Jonesboro, Arkansas;

April 1998—Fayetteville, Tennessee; April 1999—Littleton, Colorado. These dates and places—these outbreaks of mass violence and needless loss of young lives—serve as a cruel reminder of something gone wrong, desperately wrong, in a nation founded upon faith in God and a respect for His eternal commandments.

"Liberal commentators in the media, academe, and the justice system deride the notion that restoring prayer and posting the Ten Commandments can help stem the tide of violence and bloodshed. They prefer secular solutions, especially ones that involve more federal spending and regulation. In effect, they favor more concertina wire, metal detectors, and armed security guards instead of the simple and effective teaching of moral absolutes.

"Yet, teaching moral absolutes is out of the question. *'We don't want to trample on the civil rights of students.' 'We don't want to teach that one creed or one code of conduct or one lifestyle is better than another.'*

"When will they understand that secular solutions will never solve spiritual problems?

"Tragically, as in the days of the Roman Empire, we too have become accustomed to 'bread and circuses.' With our stomachs full and our minds preoccupied with the pleasures of this world, we fail to seriously ponder the reason for the tragedies that are regularly occurring before our very eyes. We rarely contemplate the significance of the judiciary's usurpation of power and suppression of religious liberty. When and if we do, we are too often afraid to take a stand—ashamed of our faith in God, afraid to hazard the notion of putting God back into the public square.

"We must not wait for more violence, for a total breakdown of our schools and our communities. We must not be silent while every vestige of God is removed from our public life and while every public display of faith is annihilated. The time has come to recover the valiant courage of our forefathers, who understood that faith and freedom are inseparable and that they are worth fighting for.

"In the words of that great Christian and patriot, Patrick Henry:

'We must fight! I repeat it, sir, we must fight! An appeal to arms and to the God of Hosts is all that is left us! . . . Why stand we here idle? What is it that the gentlemen wish? What would they have? Is life so dear, or peace so sweet, as to be purchased at the price of chains and slavery? Forbid it, Almighty God! I know not what course others may take, but as for me, give me liberty or give me death!'"

Author's Comments

My thanks to Judge Moore for his insight, his courage, his eloquence, and his permission to include his commentary in this work. Since this book is primarily aimed at the inadequacy of spiritual and moral training and guidance in our public education system, I am prompted to add my own thoughts to those of Judge Moore.

He is absolutely right in faulting some of his peers in the legal profession who have engaged in judicial activism to distort and twist the letter and intent of the U.S. Constitution. I would, however, suggest that much of the judicial activism that we mutually deplore is a reflection of the mores of our society at large, which have been shaped by the deliberate indoctrination of our children into the humanistic philosophies of Karl Marx and John Dewey.

Marx set the stage in the mid-1800s with his *Communist Manifesto*. John Dewey, as the acknowledged founder of our contemporary public education philosophies, launched the attack on traditional spiritual and moral concepts with his *Humanist Manifesto* in 1933. It was in this amoral swamp that many future members of our legal profession found their sustenance, while concurrently receiving the support of an increasing number of lay people who were indoctrinated into the same immoral religion of Humanism.

Judge Moore is right in calling for a restoration, within the legal profession, of the moral principles embodied in Judeo-Christianity. I would simply add that it is doubtful that such an honorable goal can be achieved in one generation.

It took over three generations of indoctrination into the godless world of Marx and Dewey to take us where are today. It will require at least two generations of students in a more religiously oriented education system to rescue our society from that swamp. It is doubtful that the changes that Judge Moore and I would like to see in our judicial system can occur without a change in the spiritual and moral composition of our education system and our society at large.

Like Marx and Dewey said, "It all begins in the minds of our children." It has also been said, "Tell me what our children are being taught today and I will tell you what kind of society we will have twenty-five years from now."

We cannot waste another day to meet the challenge before us.

8

The Economics of Religious Pursuit

In the preceding chapters we documented the sad state of affairs in our government-run public schools, why it has been a major factor in the moral and socioeconomic decline of our nation, and why government-run public schools are beyond redemption as long as they adhere to the amoral philosophies of Karl Marx and John Dewey. We also explained the letter, the meaning, and the intent of the First Amendment of the U.S. Constitution.

With that as background, let us continue our search for solutions by considering the important element of *economics* in the *exercise* of religion.

Economics of Religious Exercise

In nearly all cases, the "exercise" of religion involves attendance at a church, a synagogue, a mosque, etc. In the case of education of children, it involves attendance at religiously oriented schools. The exercise of God-fearing religion, as guaranteed in the First Amendment, cannot be found in public schools.

Indeed, public schools have assumed an adversarial role *against* religion to such a degree that it functions as an alienating wedge between parents and their own children who are told in public schools that the religious beliefs of their parents are not valid . . . that students should make up their own minds on religious and moral concepts.

Exercise of religion involves buildings, desks, books, computers, etc., which require substantial financial investments. The last time I checked neither church or school buildings, or the money to build, equip, and maintain them, grow on trees.

These tangible and costly facilities require personnel: pastors, priests, rabbis, teachers, administrators, custodians, etc., which also involve considerable financial outlays. Then comes overhead: maintenance, repairs, heat, light, water, office supplies, printing, etc., all of which involve more money.

☆ In short, free exercise of religion is not free!

It costs money . . . a lot of money that must be paid by those who wish to exercise their religion, including the ability to send their children to a religiously oriented school. It is not just a simple ritual of kneeling at one's bedside, or on a mountaintop.

None of that is mysterious, but it is often overlooked or disregarded in this secular world of ours.

In most families the costs of exercising and pursuing religion is a strain on already tight budgets. After paying for housing, food, clothing, medical bills, transportation, and hefty federal, state, and local taxes, there isn't enough left in most families to pay tuition at private secular or parochial schools. So children are doomed to remain in the amoral swamp of public schools.

An Analogy

With this background let's consider an analogy. Suppose a man enters your home while you are away and leaves with *all* your possessions. Would you say the man is a thief and a burglar? Of course you would. You might even have other unkind words to describe him.

Now suppose that the man enters your home while you are away and leaves with only one of your television sets. Would you still say he is a thief and a burglar? Of course you would. The fact that he did not take all your possessions does not exempt him from a charge of thievery or stealing.

Now let's apply that analogy to the economic aspects of religious exercise and the ability of parents to pay tuition for their children at a parochial school.

Suppose government were to confiscate *all* parental income via taxation, which Bastiat called "legalized plunder." Since it requires money to exercise religion, including education of children in a religious environment, we would have to agree that the State has invalidated the right of parents to exercise religion. Government has negated that guarantee by taking away from parents the funds needed to pay tuitions that are necessary for the economic viability of parochial schools.

In that case the State has interfered with, indeed prohibited, the right and ability of parents to freely exercise their religion. That would be a de facto violation of the free exercise clause of the First Amendment.

Now let's assume that the State takes only *part* of parental income . . . a part that would otherwise be used to pay tuition at a parochial school, making it difficult or impossible for parents to *freely exercise* their religious beliefs and to perpetuate those beliefs in their children.

In that event, has the State intruded upon, and interfered with, the parental right of free, unrestrained exercise of religion? Of course it has!

☆ The First Amendment makes no allowances for partial violations of its guarantees. When the State takes away any part of the money that would otherwise be used in the free exercise of religion, the State has violated the First Amendment. As we said in the analogy, a burglar is a burglar no matter how much he steals. And a government that engages in legalized plunder is guilty of that offense no matter how much it steals.

Free Exercise and Free Speech

Defenders of the First Amendment right of free speech argue loudly against *any* interference with that right, even when it is implemented in a manner offensive to most Americans, such as the obscenities that appear routinely on our motion picture and television screens, or the atrocities that appear in art museums at taxpayer expense.

☆ Why, then, should there not be similar strong objection to *any* restriction, hindrance, or interference with the ability of parents to *freely exercise* their religion, including a right to share in tax funds that they were forced to pay in order to send their children to religiously oriented schools? Has the humanistic religion of John Dewey so dulled the moral conscience of administrators, faculty, the courts, the media, and graduates of public schools that they cannot sense the degree to which the State violates the First Amendment?

Taxation and Inflation

When the First Amendment was ratified there were no income taxes, no Social Security taxes, no school district taxes, very limited property taxes, and very few other forms of taxation. Indeed, it was the minuscule taxes on British tea that resulted in the Boston Tea Party and the War for Independence.

Total federal, state, and local taxes came to less than $6.75 per capita when the U.S. Constitution was ratified. Tariffs on imports provided up to 85 percent of all revenue needed to run the federal government for the next 125 years. Those who preferred to buy American products paid virtually no federal taxes. As recently as 1915, federal, state, and local government taxes still represented less than 10 percent of national income.

Today, however, government confiscates nearly 50 percent of all privately generated income, thereby depriving most parents of the economic capability of maintaining a decent standard of living, let alone paying parochial school tuitions.

We should also understand that all taxes inevitably land in prices of consumer goods. Thus, government (the State) is also responsible for diluting, via tax-induced price inflation, the after-tax ability of parents, as consumers, to pay tuition at parochial schools.

As a result of tax-induced price inflation, the buying power of the U.S. dollar is now less than 1 percent of what it was when the Constitution was ratified; less than 5 percent of what it was in 1915; and barely 18 percent of what it was worth as recently as 1960.

According to the Consumer Price Index, as contained in the "1999 Economic Report of the President to Congress," what cost $2.96 in 1960 now costs $16.30. A loaf of plain white bread that cost 10 cents in 1960 now costs at least $1.25. A car that cost $1,795 in 1960 now costs over $10,000.

Trade Policies Restrict Parental Economic Ability

This squeeze on parental economic ability has been exacerbated by U.S. foreign trade policies that violate basic principles of moral ethics, the U.S. Constitution, and economic laws.

Contrary to a general perception that we have free trade within the U.S., we have literally millions of federal, state, and local regulatory and tax laws, judicial rulings, and monetary edicts that are responsible for over 80 percent of the cost of the average American product or service. Taxes alone, which totaled $2.7 trillion in 1998, add at least 50 percent to product costs attributable to true private endeavor.

Being subjected to these tremendous cost burdens as U.S. companies and employees, we have reason to presume that a moral government would protect every U.S. company and employee against any competitors, including foreign producers, who do not abide by similar political mandates and who absorb similar cost burdens. But that is not the case. Instead, U.S. trade policies, such as GATT, WTO, NAFTA, MFN-for-China, CBI, etc., encourage importation of products from foreign producers who do not abide by similar standards, and whose products are made under conditions that are contrary to nearly all U.S. laws, plus cultural and monetary standards.

As a result of this double-standard policy, the U.S. suffered over $2.6 trillion in trade deficits since 1971. Over four thousand U.S. factories were shut down. Factory and office expansions were shifted to other countries. Over 20 million workers lost their jobs. Industrial urban areas were decimated. Our tax base was sabotaged, resulting in a $5.2 trillion increase in federal debt from $408 billion in 1971 to $5.6 trillion in 1998.

This, in turn, forced the federal government to pay over $240 billion a year in interest to private lenders, including over $70 billion to foreigners. That, in turn, required the average U.S. household to pay an additional $2,200 in higher taxes to cover that interest burden, plus higher consumer prices as those taxes and higher interest rates impacted costs of producing consumer needs.

One example of the duplicity that saturates U.S trade policies is reflected in our minimum-wage laws. Whereas the federal government mandates that every worker be paid a minimum of $5.15 an hour, U.S. trade policies pit them against the lowest wage and living standards in the world . . . less than $1 an hour in China, Malaysia, Mexico, India, Bangladesh, Indonesia, etc., in violation of the equal protection clause of the Fourteenth Amendment.

As a consequence of this double-dealing, the wages of average American working people, when adjusted for inflation and taxes, in 1997 were 20 percent *below* 1971. These factors, in turn, literally tore our social fabric apart. Millions of wives and mothers were forced to go to work to provide a second income, in order to maintain reasonable living standards. This, in turn, resulted in over 8 million latchkey children who have no parent to come home to after school, no parent to provide the counsel and support every child needs.

In summary, numerous studies reveal that the polarization gap between rich and poor is now wider that at any time in U.S. history, thereby making it increasingly more difficult for parents to pay tuition for the education of their children at private secular or parochial schools.

Surely, anyone with a moral conscience should be able to sense the immorality and the unconstitutionality of such trade policies and their debilitating effect on our social order. Yet as a result of our amoral education system in the past fifty years, the majority of Americans do not comprehend it.

The State Is Responsible

Thus, as a result of rising taxes, tax-induced price inflation, and immoral trade policies, the State has been responsible for the dissipation of a major share of parental income that could otherwise be used to pay tuitions at parochial schools. The reader should also consider monetary policies (usurious interest rates) and excessive immigration that have further depressed the economic capability of average working Americans.

☆ None of these circumstances were even remotely in evidence when the First Amendment was written. If our

Founding Fathers could see what has happened in the last fifty years, they would soon put an end to the travesty and the fraud that now prevails.

☆ They would say: "Of what value is the Constitutional guarantee of free exercise of religion when the state takes away all, or any part, of its economic life-blood, and uses it to create an economic wall that stands as an adversarial barrier to the fulfillment of that guarantee? In so doing, the State has made a mockery of the First Amendment."

Government as a Giant Adversary

Lest the reader still fail to grasp the significance of what has been said thus far, let us now consider the massive impact of government intrusion in our education system and the manner in which it functions as a giant adversary against the free exercise of religion. Through its economic power and its self-ordained bureaucratic powers, the State has changed the intent of the First Amendment from "freedom *of* religion" to "freedom *from* and *against* religion."

As mentioned earlier, federal, state, and local governments in 1998 confiscated over $320 billion from U.S. citizens to fund public elementary and secondary education, plus another $150 billion for higher education, for a total of $470 billion. That figures out to $4,700 per household, and $7,700 per student enrolled in our government school system: $6,100 per K–12 student and $12,000 per college student.

☆ This massive intrusion on parental economic ability is for the exclusive purpose of funding a government-run public school system that millions of parents do not want!

The tyranny in this instance is infinitely greater than the tyranny of King George that led to the Boston Tea Party, the

Declaration of Independence, and the Revolutionary War. All that pales into insignificance compared to the tyranny now taking place by our government school system . . . a tyranny deliberately aimed at shaping the minds of children to conform with the agenda of the *Humanist Manifesto* as promulgated by John Dewey, and a powerful and corrupt elite.

The tyranny then puts parents in the untenable, often impossible, position of paying additional money to send their kids to a school they *do* want them to attend. But, it is money they no longer have because government took it away from them in a process of plunder and legalized theft.

- ☆ By allocating all of these funds to government schools, euphemistically called "public" schools, and denying any of those funds to parochial schools, the "state" compounds its usurpation of the First Amendment by also violating the equal protection clause of the Fourteenth Amendment, which mandates that all laws and government programs be applied equally so that no citizen is placed in the category of a second-class citizen. We are all supposed to be equal under the law.
- ☆ The State protects public schools to the detriment of parochial schools, which are denied equal protection, even though religious pursuit is protected under the Constitution whereas a government school system is not. Indeed, there is not a word in the Constitution that even remotely authorizes an establishment of a public school system founded on the humanistic religion of John Dewey. By denying religiously oriented parents the right to share in education funds, to which they have contributed under force of tax law, those parents and their children are, in fact, relegated to second-class citizens simply because they confess a belief in God and desire to exercise their right to have their children educated in a spiritual and moral environment.

☆ According to *West's Encyclopedia of American Law*, 1998, in *Sherbert v. Verner* (1963) the Supreme Court held that "a law that places an indirect burden on the practice of religion so as to impede the observance of religion, or a law that discriminates between religions, is unconstitutional."

When any money earned by private citizens is confiscated and then allocated to only one form of education to the detriment of religiously oriented parents and their children, the State is guilty of making a mockery of the equal protection clause of the Fourteenth Amendment.

If there is to be a "separation of church and state," the first priority is for the State to cease and desist from interfering in the financial ability of parents to send their children to a parochial school. Under present circumstances the State is guilty of violating the free exercise clause, the establishment clause, and the equal protection clause of the Constitution.

The State Uses Confiscated Money to Finance the Religion of Humanism

This should not be viewed as a frivolous interpretation of the First Amendment. The *Humanist Manifesto* itself clearly identifies its theories and beliefs as a religion that rejects reverence for God or any Supreme Being. Since that is the philosophy of the government school system, as promulgated by John Dewey and the National Education Association, it becomes clear that all of the $470 billion now being confiscated from U.S. citizens under the flag of education is for the purpose of establishing a state religion known as Humanism.

☆ The basic difference between the state religion now in vogue in U.S. public schools and the state religion in seventeenth-century England is that the English system recognized God and the U.S. system does not!

In that context, it is quite apparent that our government school system routinely acts *against* God-fearing religions. That is in violation of the establishment clause, which says that government shall make no laws with respect to, or with regard to, religion . . . neither for or *against*!

The State Nullifies First Amendment Guarantees

The situation is grotesque! By allocating all educational funds to government schools, the State acts as a giant adversary *against* every other system of schools, including parochial schools. This constitutes a government action "with respect to an establishment of religion" contrary to the First Amendment, which says government "shall make no laws respecting an establishment of religion." In this case, the State has made laws with respect to religion . . . not to advance religion, but to *destroy* God-fearing religion and to nullify First Amendment guarantees.

That indictment was underscored on October 12, 1999, when the Supreme Court denied a State of Maine plan to issue vouchers so children could go to religious schools. Rev. Barry Lynn, of Americans United for Separation of Church and State, said the Court's denial pleased him most. He said, as reported by the Associated Press: "It's a victory of sorts because it establishes that the taxpayers of Maine do not have to fund religious schools. Parents can create religious schools but cannot get everyone to pay for them."

American Indians of bygone days had a word for that kind of talk: "White man speak with forked tongue." *Lynn neglected to say that taxpayers in Maine are forced to pay for an antireligious school system they do not want!* Yet they are denied use of any of those funds so their children can be educated in the moral environment provided by religiously oriented schools. By denying that right to parents and their children, Lynn and the Supreme Court trampled on the equal protection clause of the Fourteenth Amendment, as well as the establishment and free exercise clauses of the First Amendment.

Lynn's strident hostility toward parochial schools is typical of his past statements. By using the title of "Reverend" he attempts to give his utterances credibility. The last time such duplicity made history was about two thousand years ago in an event known as the "Last Supper," when Jesus said that one of his disciples would betray him. That disciple's name was Judas.

The State Engages in Duplicity

Let's assume for a moment that the "separation of church and state" cliché is valid. That would imply that the State should maintain a hands-off approach to all matters of religion, including its economic viability. That would require the State to avoid taking money away from religiously oriented people that would otherwise be used in the free exercise of religion.

If the State uses those plundered funds for a public school system that parents do *not* want, the State has constructed an arbitrary one-way street to the detriment of parents who prefer that their money be used for tuitions at schools that instruct their children in a religious environment and the moral principles embodied therein.

In that event, the State has clearly violated the "separation of church and state" red herring that its advocates, like Rev. Lynn, keep bringing up.

☆ The religious community does not ask for aid to implement the free exercise guarantee. Rather, it simply asks that the State either stop confiscating the money from them in the first place, or allow them to share in those funds in a manner that would be consistent with the free exercise clause and the equal protection clause.

The State Stands Between Parents and Children

The adversarial stance of public schools applies not only to economic considerations, but also as it thrusts upon its students concepts diametrically opposed to religious beliefs, and the moral principles emanating therefrom. In that manner government schools function as a wedge between parents and their own children, making them even more rebellious to parental guidance and supervision. Surely, this kind of intrusion in the family structure was never intended or envisioned by our Founding Fathers.

What is a child to think when told in a government school that what he or she is taught in church or in the home is wrong? What is a child to think when told that church and parental opposition to sex relations outside the bonds of matrimony, abortions, homosexuality, unequal application of laws in double-standard trade policies, etc., is wrong? What are children to think when government schools give condoms to children, contrary to admonitions by parents against sexual promiscuity?

When a child is taught creationism or other religious concepts in the home or church, but is exposed to specific teachings to the contrary in government schools, the State competes *against*, and *interferes with*, the rights of parents to freely exercise religion. The State is then guilty of establishing its own religion of Humanism in the minds of naïve children, contrary to the wishes of their parents.

The issue is not whether creationism or evolution is correct. The issue is whether the First Amendment right to freely exercise religion is to be honored, or whether government may establish its own Humanism religion in the minds of children against the wishes of their parents.

When a child is taught in church or the home such basic principles as the Ten Commandments, but is told in government schools, to a point of ridicule, that the U.S. Constitution forbids any discussion, or any recognition, of the Ten Commandments, government functions as an adversary against the rights of parents to freely exercise their religion and to perpetuate it through their children.

To suggest otherwise is to also suggest that the State has higher rights and responsibilities with respect to children than do their own parents, thereby undermining the ability of parents to assume full responsibility for the development and actions of their own children. Unfortunately, that is the direction in which our public schools and government bureaucrats are leading us. Indeed, that is what Hillary Rodham Clinton was advocating when she wrote that "it takes a village to raise a child." In other words, government has greater rights with respect to children than their own parents.

☆ Yet when students go on shooting rampages, and undertake other forms of violence, parents are accused of not assuming their responsibilities, with no recognition of the fact that government schools have usurped those responsibilities and prerogatives.

Yoder v. Wisconsin

In the late '60s and early '70s, Yoder, an Amish parent, refused to send his children to Wisconsin public high schools because of their antireligious teachings. The State of Wisconsin sued Yoder in an attempt to force him to send his children to public schools until the age of sixteen. The Wisconsin Supreme Court ruled in favor of Yoder.

Not satisfied, public school bureaucrats in Wisconsin filed an appeal with the U.S. Supreme Court. Fortunately, the Court, in Case No. 6598, acted on March 29, 1971, saying "certiorari denied," meaning that the case was not accepted for review, thereby letting stand the Wisconsin Supreme Court's decision in Yoder's favor.

It was a clear endorsement of the contention that government schools do infringe on the rights of parents to raise their children in a religious environment . . . and that parents do have a right to refuse to let their children be exposed to the humanistic religion of John Dewey and Karl Marx.

The State vs. America

It should be disconcerting to every American that the socialistic and antireligion manifestos of Marx and Dewey have become so ingrained in the minds and actions of thousands, perhaps millions, of people on government payrolls (including teachers, administrators, politicians, bureaucrats, even Supreme Court judges) that they function as a virtual army to carry out the Marx/Dewey agenda.

For example, Nebraska State Senator Peter Hoagland said, "Fundamental, Bible-believing people do not have the right to indoctrinate their children in their beliefs because we, the state, are preparing them for the year 2000 when America will be part of a one-world global society and their children will not fit in."

While that statement may appear preposterous, it is the underlying philosophy of government schools, their teachers, and administrators. I am a personal witness to that process. I have four granddaughters, each of whom graduated from public schools in suburban Seattle between 1982 and 1986. I attended all graduation ceremonies.

In every instance, school officials and student valedictorians spoke glowingly of "going on to make this a better *world*." Never once was it intimated that the students might try to make *America* a better country, to honor our Constitution, to follow the path of freedom laid out by our Founding Fathers, many of whom gave their lives in that great cause. No, it was all about advancing global socialism and the new world order.

When I protested to school administrators, I was told I was "old-fashioned . . . We are now citizens of the *world*." When I asked, "In what country are you a citizen and to what country do you owe your allegiance?" I got blank stares and bureaucratic brushoffs.

The U.S. Declares War on Parochial Schools

The havoc inflicted on religiously oriented schools by the State is difficult to fully document. However, Catholic schools, which have represented the majority of parochial schools since the end of World War II, do provide credible evidence. I am not a member of the Catholic Church, but I have great respect for it, as I do for all God-fearing religions. So, from that ecumenical vantage point, let's look at some data.

As recently as 1960, there were 12,893 Catholic elementary and secondary schools. By 1996, there were only 8,231. A net 4,662 Catholic schools had closed: 36.2 percent of the number existing just thirty-six years earlier.

In 1960, there were 5,273,000 students enrolled in Catholic elementary and secondary schools. By 1996, there were only 2,664,000 students in Catholic schools, a reduction of 2,609,000 students: a decrease of nearly 50 percent at the same time that U.S. population increased 85 million or 47 percent.

In 1960, there were 36,227,000 students enrolled in K–12 government schools. By 1996, this number had soared to 45,630,000: an *increase* of 26 percent in the same time span that Catholic school enrollment *fell* 50 percent!

Whereas Catholic K–12 schools accounted for 14.5 percent of elementary and secondary school enrollment in 1960, it represented only 5.7 percent by 1996.

In 1997, private and parochial schools spent about $3,800 per average daily K–12 student, whereas public schools spent $6,100 per student: 61 percent more! At the same time, classroom teachers in private and parochial schools, who relied on *voluntary contributions*, were paid an average of barely $24,000 a year compared with public school teachers who, relying on confiscatory taxation, averaged $40,133 a year: 67 percent more.

Against the weight of such economic imbalances, it is a near miracle that parochial schools can exist at all. It should not be surprising, therefore, that they have closed at an alarming rate, and under present policies are threatened with annihilation. In that event, government (the State) would have to assume full responsibility for absolute violation of the First Amendment guarantee of free exercise of religion.

☆ The State is not just letting it happen; it is making it happen!

Spending Goes Up As Quality Goes Down

In view of the foregoing economic comparisons it would be natural to assume that government schools are turning out far superior students. But the facts, as revealed earlier and as documented by many studies, tell us that government schools are turning out vastly inferior students, not only with respect to academic subjects, but in the far more important context of morality.

It is abundantly clear that government schools are turning out students with little or no sense of moral values, who are ill-equipped to provide the kind of moral input and leadership that our social, economic, and political order so desperately needs. Yet these products of a morally bankrupt government school system sit as judges in our courts of jurisprudence, including the U.S. Supreme Court, making decisions that trash time-honored moral standards and the U.S. Constitution.

By instituting economic policies that place the confiscatory power of government in competition against religiously oriented schools that are funded by voluntary contributions, there should be no doubt that the State, whether by deliberate design, or unwitting actions, has assumed a gigantic adversarial stance *against* religion in violation of the First Amendment.

This stance has been aided and abetted by the insidious and pervasive support of a liberal media even as it argues in favor of free speech to serve its own interests. Most proposals to seek realistic solutions to our social and economic problems are promptly shot down by media editors, most of whom are graduates of public schools and who, as such, find it difficult to distinguish right from wrong in many issues.

The economic force of an adversarial government school system, its ruinous effect on religious education, and the decline of moral standards in America should now be evident.

The State Violates Separation of Church and State

Contrary to allegations that religion has violated "separation of church and state" principles, it is clear that the reverse is true. The State has blatantly violated that cliché and the First Amendment of the U.S. Constitution.

Far from any intrusion by the Church in the affairs of the State, the State has scaled the walls of the Church to a point that the First Amendment has been tossed into a trash bin.

9

U.S. Supreme Court Fumbles the Football Case

As the final manuscript for this book was being prepared, the United States Supreme Court, on June 19, 2000, removed all doubt about its hostility toward religion. It fumbled the "football case."

The case is known as *Santa Fe Independent School District v. Jane Doe, 99–62*. In it the Court ruled that student-led prayers at high school football games, in a suburb of Houston, Texas, violated the U.S. Constitution. The rationale used by the Court, in a 6–3 majority opinion, written by Justice John Paul Stevens, was one of the most convoluted ever to come down from the high court. Justices O'Connor, Kennedy, Souter, Breyer, and Ginsburg concurred with Stevens.

Instead of relying directly on the letter and intent of specific language in the First Amendment, Stevens's opinion relied almost exclusively on prior court rulings that departed from the original intent of our Constitution, including emphasis on a 1992 case in which the court barred clergy-led prayers, invocations, and benedictions at public school graduation ceremonies.

It was reminiscent of an old vaudeville routine where a person tells a story to a second person, who then tells it to a third person, who tells it to a fourth person, ad infinitum, until it reaches the tenth person, at which point the story is nothing like the original version. In like manner, through tainted case law on top of tainted case law, the high court has thoroughly trashed the handiwork of our Founding Fathers to a point that its implementation is nothing like its original and intended version.

The decision prompted Chief Justice William H. Rehnquist to write, in a dissenting opinion shared by Justices Antonin Scalia and Clarence Thomas, that "he found the tone of the court's opinion more disturbing than its substance. It bristles with hostility to all things religious in public life."

Instead of abiding by the First Amendment right of every person to "freely exercise religion, without restriction or interference," Stevens's opinion seemed to be more concerned with how student-led prayers at a football game might be perceived by members of the audience who hold no reverence for a Supreme Being, even to the extent of bigotry, or who have little or no comprehension of what the First Amendment says and intends.

For example: The majority opinion itself; comments by various individuals who were opposed to such prayers; and opinions of media reporters, columnists, and editors reflect a prevailing belief that prayers by students at a football game violate "the Constitutionally required separation of church and state," or as some phrased it, "the separation of government and religion."

But, of course, as has been thoroughly documented throughout this work, there is no such stipulation in the U.S. Constitution. Instead, the First Amendment is a restriction on what government can do, not on what religious people or organizations can do. Thus, the majority opinion in the Santa Fe football case rests on language and intent that is nowhere to be found in the Constitution. The responsibility of the Supreme Court is to the U.S. Constitution, not some convoluted phraseology that does not appear in that sacred document.

Whereas the First Amendment erects an imaginary wall that is not to be scaled by any branch of government with respect to religion, the free exercise clause and the free speech clause—all in the same sentence as the establishment clause—guarantee to every citizen the unrestricted, unhampered right to scale that wall by exercising their religion, including expressing their views and beliefs in the political realm and in the public square. The free speech clause further guarantees that right.

Should anyone infer that the free exercise clause is not applicable in public buildings or on other public properties, I would simply ask: "Show me where the Constitution imposes such restrictions." There is none! Instead, the entire text of the First Amendment, in context, means: "Congress (and by extension any government agency) shall not make any law or edict that would prohibit the free exercise of religion." The word "free," which means without restrictions, qualifications, or penalties, says it all.

The First Amendment is intended to protect and guarantee religious freedom . . . and to *exercise* it! It is *not* the purpose of the First Amendment to protect government-run public schools, or individuals and organizations who reflect bigotry, animosity, and hostility toward God-fearing religions. The First Amendment was *not* written to protect and advance the religion of Humanism as set forth in the *Humanist Manifesto* of John Dewey, the agenda of the National Education

Association, or the *Communist Manifesto* of Karl Marx, all of which are imbedded in the core philosophy of public schools.

The *Santa Fe* case found its origin in a student-initiated desire to say a prayer at football games, over the public-address system, on behalf of the players and spectators. The first occasion involved a young lady who, in deference to her right of privacy, will be identified here only as Jane Doe, who subsequently became the target of a suit by the American Civil Liberties Union (ACLU), an organization known for its hostility toward religion, especially Christianity.

The inference in Stevens's majority opinion, and in subsequent comments by antireligion groups and the liberal media, is that by "allowing" the student to say a prayer at the football games, the Santa Fe School Board became a "sponsor" of a religion contrary to their convoluted interpretation of the establishment clause of the First Amendment.

Of course, if the School Board *did initiate* the prayer, by ordering the students to say a prayer, it would be proper to say that the School Board became its sponsor . . . and the Court would be correct in finding that the School Board entered the forbidden zone of "establishing or promoting a specific religion."

But that is not what happened! The idea of saying a prayer at the games was initiated by the students. In that event the school (being a government entity) could not "disallow" or "forbid" the students from doing so. If it did, it would be "making a law with respect to religion," an act that the establishment clause forbids it to do.

The establishment clause imposes a limitation on what government can do, i.e., it should not pass any "law or edict" with regard to religion, whether it be "for or against" religion. By remaining neutral in the matter, and "allowing" the students to engage in a prayer, the School Board would be acting in the manner specified by the First Amendment, i.e., it would be "allowing" the free exercise rights of the students.

If the school said "no" to the student initiative it would violate the free exercise and the free speech clauses which provide a guarantee to students, as for all Americans, of the right to exercise religious thoughts and words at any time and any place. The free exercise clause does not limit its guarantee by saying "except on public property, such as a public school or park." It poses no limitation of any kind on the free exercise of religion.

Moreover, public property is the property of "We, the People" who paid the taxes to acquire and maintain that property. To say that taxpayers and their children cannot use property they paid for is as preposterous as saying a member of a club who regularly pays his dues is not entitled to use the facilities of the club.

Therefore, every branch of government must be sure that its edicts do *not* deny access to, or use of, public property by "The People," especially when such rights are specifically protected by the free exercise clause of the First Amendment.

Thus, if the Santa Fe School Board were to disallow the student request to offer a prayer at the football games it would be making a law against religion, contrary to the establishment, free exercise, and free speech clauses. The First Amendment clearly forbids any branch of government from doing so.

Thus, the Court's majority ruling finds no support in the U.S. Constitution. The text of Justice Stevens's opinion is a convoluted assemblage of legal gobbledygook based on tainted prior decisions that reflect mounting judicial hostility toward religion. The Court seemed more concerned with freedom "from" religion than with freedom "of" religion as guaranteed in the First Amendment.

The Court misinterpreted the establishment clause as it has on numerous prior occasions. As stated in chapter 6 the phrase "an establishment" is a noun that describes an entity, form, or expression of religion. But this latest Court ruling misinterprets that clause to infer that the phrase is a verb by giving it the meaning of an action taken by government to establish, install, or favor a specific religion. But that is not what the establishment clause says.

To give it the meaning and intent implied by the Court, the clause would have to read "Congress shall make no law respecting *the* establishment of *a* religion." By changing the word "an" to "the" and inserting the word "a" before "religion," the word "establishment" becomes similar to an action verb. If that were the case it would be a flat-out restriction on government from establishing, installing, aiding, or favoring any form or expression of religion.

But that is not the way the establishment clause is written. Being a noun it forbids any branch of government from enacting *any* law or ruling "with regard to, or with respect to" an entity, form, or expression of religion, whether it be for or against religion. That would apply to tangible brick-and-mortar buildings, like churches, or the intangible exercise of religion, such as a prayer at a football game . . . or to open sessions of Congress as has been its practice since the first Congress met in 1789.

Is the Court in the *Santa Fe* case saying the framers of the Constitution, and the Congress that ratified it, didn't know what they were doing when they authorized a Chaplain to say a prayer at the first session of Congress and each session thereafter? Surely, the Court cannot be so presumptuous and arrogant.

And so, if it is consistent with the intent of the framers of our Constitution to open each session of Congress with an invocation or prayer, by what standard did the Court conclude that students cannot do likewise at a football game, unless it was to reflect their ever-increasing hostility to all things religious?

By misinterpreting the establishment clause, the Court "made a law with respect to religion," an act that is expressly forbidden by the establishment clause, whether the law be for or against religion.

U.S. Supreme Court Fumbles the Football Case

In the final analysis, the Supreme Court placed itself in an untenable position by entertaining the *Santa Fe* case. Regardless of how the Court ruled, for or against, it would be making a law with respect to religion, which is a violation of the establishment clause, as well as the free exercise and free speech clauses.

The error of the Court's ruling in the *Santa Fe* case was confirmed by a public opinion poll conducted via the Internet by American Online, immediately following the Court's announcement on the morning of June 19, 2000. AOL asked its subscribers to vote "yes," "no," or "not sure" on the following question: "Do you think a student-led prayer violates the Constitutionally required separation of government and religion?"

By 9:45 P.M. Pacific Daylight Time, 26,896 people had cast their vote. The great number who voted in such a short time, in itself, reflected an overwhelming distaste for the Court's decision. Here is how they voted:

YES	7,435	27.6%
NO	18,914	70.3%
NOT SURE	547	2.0%
TOTAL	26,896	99.9%

The overwhelming 70.3 percent opinion that the Court erred is all the more remarkable considering that the question was phrased in a manner that implied that the Constitution mandates the "separation of government and religion." This may have prompted some to vote "yes." But, as underscored throughout this book, there is no such stipulation in the Constitution. Thus, some who assumed that the question was correctly stated may have overinflated the number of "yes" votes.

The poll results are also remarkable in the very small percentage who said they were "not sure." Apparently, the average American is better informed on what the Constitution says and intends than a majority on the Supreme Court who answered "yes" to the AOL question.

We should not leave this review of the *Santa Fe* football case without reaffirming that the manner in which the U.S. public school system is founded and administered violates the Constitution. Thus, the case turned into a case of the pot calling the kettle black.

The public school system is not only constructed in a manner that violates the Constitution (as documented in chapter 8), it is morally bankrupt as was documented in the early chapters of this book. So we have an utterly ridiculous situation whereby an illegal, unconstitutional school system is being used by the Court as a means of "making another law against an establishment of religion and against the free exercise of religion."

By coercively taxing all citizens, including those who are opposed to concepts taught in public schools, through a process the French economist Frederic Bastiat called "legalized theft," and then denying religiously oriented parents the right to share in those funds by enrolling their children in a parochial school, the state not only violates the First Amendment but also the equal protection clause of the Fourteenth Amendment.

How, then, dare a government that violates the U.S. Constitution say that a student cannot say a prayer at a football game!

This is tantamount to the Mafia defining the rules of civil conduct, or a pack of wolves setting the rules on how to maintain law and order in a chicken coop.

How dare a corrupt government, and a corrupt judicial system, deny a high school student the right to say a prayer at a football game!

If there ever was a judicial verdict that reflected the moral bankruptcy of our judicial system, Supreme Court Justice John Paul Stevens's majority opinion in the case of *Santa Fe Independent School District v. Jane Doe* is prima facie evidence.

Case closed!

10

The Church and State Are Not Separate

In preceding chapters we examined the letter and intent of the First Amendment. We exploded the myth of "separation of church and state." We provided conclusive evidence of the manner in which the State, through its economic powers, has constructed a wall that stands as a barrier to the fulfillment of the guarantees contained in the Constitution of the United States.

To add emphasis and validity to what has already been said, let us now consider the testimony of Dr. D. James Kennedy before the Subcommittee of the Senate Judiciary Committee on June 26, 1984. Dr. Kennedy is the senior minister of the Coral Ridge, Florida, Presbyterian Church and president and speaker of the Coral Ridge Ministries Television and Radio programs.

With his permission, here is an excerpt of his testimony:

"There are today several ominous movements going on in America and in the Western world, for the most part undetected by Christians, which . . . portend great evil for the church unless we understand them and do something about them. There is, first of all, a tremendous change that is coming about in the relationship of the church and the state in America. It is happening so slowly that we are like that frog sitting in the pot of warm water which is gradually being heated to the boiling point. The frog just sits there and is slowly boiled to death. Like the frog, we do not even perceive what is happening. We have today, dominant in this country and accepted by 99 percent of the people, a view of the relationship of church and state which is almost diametrically opposite to that which was taught by the Founding Fathers of this country and which was expressed in the First Amendment of our Constitution. Yet, how many people are aware of that? If it goes unchecked much further it will, as it is beginning to do right now, bring about the destruction of the liberties of Christians in this land!

The First Amendment

"Does the First Amendment teach the separation of church and state? I venture to say that 95 percent of the people in America today have been brainwashed into the place where they would say 'yes.' But it does not! I think it is vital that we understand what the First Amendment to the Constitution says, because the relationship between these two 'kingdoms' has been a long and difficult one. The Founding Fathers . . . resolved that question in a marvelous way but it is being completely destroyed in our time—and most people are not even aware of it. The First Amendment states: 'Congress shall make no law respecting an establishment of religion or prohibiting the free exercise thereof.' . . . It says nothing about the church! . . . The First Amendment *teaches the separation of the state from the church!*

"The First Amendment is a *one-way street*. It restrains the federal government. The Bill of Rights was written to restrain the federal government from interfering with the liberties of the people, because they were afraid that the people of this new country would not accept the new Constitution unless the rights of the people were further defined and protected. A 'wall of separation,' on the other hand, is most emphatically a *two-way street*. It prohibits and restrains those on one side of the wall equally as much as it restrains those on the other side of the wall. Now we have a two-way street. But in the last several decades what has been happening? It has been turned around until now we again have virtually a one-way street moving in *the opposite direction*, so that 98 percent of the time in the last year . . . when you heard the phrase 'separation of church and state' what was being discussed was: What the *church shall or shall not do*. That's 180 degrees off from the First Amendment . . . ! Now the federal government is unshackling itself from the First Amendment, and the shackles are being put on the Church!

"Legislating Morality

"Another ominous tendency is seen in the silent legal revolution going on in the Western world today. How many times have you heard it said that you can't legislate morality? Hitler was right! You can tell the big lie so often and so loud that people will come to believe it: 'You can't legislate morality!' Like the separation of church and state, I am sure that the vast majority of Americans would say to that statement, 'Of course you can't!' But I would simply . . . ask this question, my friend: 'If you can't legislate morality, pray tell me what can you legislate?' Immorality? The fact is that you cannot legislate anything but morality! We have laws against murder because it is immoral to murder; we have laws against stealing because it is immoral to steal; we have laws against rape because it is immoral to rape. This country's legislative enactments were founded incontrovertibly upon the Judeo-Christian ethic of the Founding Fathers of this country. Even Thomas Jefferson, who . . . was the least evangelical of the founders of this country, said in his Charter for the University of Virginia, that the proofs for God as the sovereign Lord and Creator and Ruler of this world and of the moral requirements and obligations which flow from that, must be taught to all students. The legislation of this country was based upon Christian morality as revealed in the Word of God. This is where we derived our morality.

"Secular Humanism

"However, for the last four decades we have seen in this nation that the Christian morality is slowly being replaced by the secular humanist morality as the foundation for legislative enactments. When that substitution is complete you will find yourself living in an America very alien from anything that you have known. When all of their so-called ethical agenda has successfully been transformed into legislation this will be a different country than ever it was before. Such things as abortion, . . .

The Church and State Are Not Separate 135

infanticide, homosexuality, free divorce, euthanasia, gambling, pornography, and suicide are . . . a portion of the . . . agenda of the secular humanist, along with the . . . complete removal of every . . . public vestige of Christian faith and religion and belief in God that has made this country great. That is their agenda and they are eagerly and determinately and assiduously engaged in enacting it as the foundation of this country's legislation under the false teaching that the government of the United States is supposed to be neutral concerning God. They are taking the concept that we are not to have an established Church and moving from that to the concept that the government is neutral concerning God.

"That is a concept . . . worse than heathenism because even heathenism is based upon the belief in some deity! All government is based upon some religious or anti-religious system. What that means for us today . . . is a very serious matter. This nation was never meant to be neutral toward God. James Madison, who wrote the Constitution, said that we cannot govern without God and the Ten Commandments. Now the Supreme Court, in its great wisdom, has said that the Ten Commandments cannot be put up on the walls of the schools of Kentucky—yet they are carved on the walls of the Supreme Court building! And the man who wrote the Constitution that they are interpreting said that we cannot govern without them!

"George Washington said it would be impossible to govern without God and the Bible. The founders of this nation never intended for this to be a nation which was neutral toward God. They did not hesitate to call upon God. They did not hesitate to mention God in their public utterances and in public buildings. They did not hesitate at all to make mention of Him or offer thanksgiving to Him for His goodness and providence, or to set aside special days of praise and prayer and thanksgiving to God, or establish chaplaincies for the Senate and House of Representatives and the Armed Services.

Separation of Church and State?

"Now we are moving irresistibly toward the Soviet-Communist concept of separation of church and state, and that is very, very dangerous. The Soviets pride[d] themselves on the fact that they believe in the separation of church and state, and America is moving rapidly to adopt their view. What is their view? It is simply this: the church is free to do anything that the government is not engaged in—and the government is engaged in almost everything! Therefore, the church is free to stay within its four walls, pray, and sing hymns, and if it does anything else it is in big trouble.

"That is what is happening in America and, unfortunately, many churches and pastors and Christians are accepting it and even defending it! It is the same sort of defeatist approach that we have taken toward the containment of Communism for the last forty years; that is, we have adopted the Communist view of our government toward religion. Remember what they said? The Communists said that what's mine is mine and what yours is negotiable. And now that is what our government is saying! They are saying, What is ours is ours and it is political; therefore, it is out of bounds for you. And what is yours is negotiable because what is religious today and spiritual today may be political tomorrow when we rule it to be legal. For example: abortion, homosexuality, suicide, or anything else. When that happens, it is like the churches in California who were asked to sign statements, such as: "Have you made any statements in the past year concerning such *political* matters as abortion, homosexuality, etc. What's mine is mine and what's yours is negotiable and we're going to negotiate you right into a little tiny closet! American Christians are sitting around just letting it happen, like the proverbial frog. And do you know why? Because we're afraid—we're afraid of the flak; we're afraid of the controversy. We've run and we've hid under our beds. We've forgotten the words of Scripture: 'Fear not.' Gentlemen, if you are going to be leaders, one thing that is called for is courage. I want to tell you, the secular humanists have declared war on Christianity in this country and . . . they are winning the war.

"Humanism is a religion. This is declared nine times in the *Humanist Manifesto* of 1933, and the second *Humanist Manifesto* in 1973. It is declared repeatedly that it is a religion. The dictionary declares it to be a religion. The secular humanists declare it to be a religion. The Supreme Court in *Torcaso v. Watkins* has declared that secular humanism is one of the several non-theistic religions operating in this country. You don't have to believe in God to have a religion. Buddhism is nontheistic, as is Taoism, as is ethical culturism—these are some nontheistic religions, according to the Supreme Court. Yet . . . humanism with its tenets of atheism, evolution, amorality, socialism, and one-world government, is taught in virtually all the public schools of this country. Therefore, secular humanism has become an established religion in this country over the last several decades, primarily through the work of such men as John Dewey and other signers of the secular *Humanist Manifesto.* It has become the established religion of America. Last year $31 billion plus was spent by the

federal government on our public educational system with its establishment of the religion of secular humanism. The Supreme Court has declared that our schools cannot teach any religion, yet the same Supreme Court has declared that secular humanism is a religion!"

Dr. Kennedy's testimony was delivered to the Senate Committee in 1984. As this is written over fifteen years have elapsed, and it is appropriate to weigh the truth and significance of what he said.

Dr. Kennedy compared what was happening in America at that time to the concept of Communism in the Soviet Union. Since then the Soviet Union has collapsed. The Berlin Wall came down in 1991. In spite of considerable effort to restore democracy, including over $20 billion of aid from the World Bank, the International Monetary Fund, and the U.S. Treasury, its now-separate states, like Russia, are in utter ruin.

A brutal war has prevailed in Russia vs. Chechnya for over five years. Their ruble is almost worthless in the global arena. Their treasury is bankrupt and unable to pay the wages of government workers . . . even military personnel. Millions of people are without jobs and income. Corruption is rampant, so much so that President Boris Yeltsin, in his resignation speech, broke down in tears and apologized for the failures of his administration.

Meanwhile, former President Ronald Reagan has been credited with—indeed virtually immortalized for—bringing the Cold War threat of the "Evil Empire" to an end. His challenge, "Mr. Gorbachev, bring down that wall," is etched in his legacy. For that his conservative legions contend that Reagan was, perhaps, the greatest president in American history, deserving of a place on Mt. Rushmore, and being responsible for all the good things that have happened to our country since he left the White House, including a seven-year "economic boom."

Although I voted for Ronald Reagan in 1980, and founded a PAC organization in San Diego to help him defeat Jimmy Carter in the election that year, I must hasten to disagree with the notion that Reagan, and only Reagan, was responsible for the collapse of the "Evil Empire." While he, unquestionably, played a part in that piece of history by his policies to strengthen our military capacity, and his firmness in dealing with Soviet leaders, that, in the final analysis, is *not* what brought about the collapse and breakup of the Soviet Union.

The fact is that the Soviet Union collapsed from within.

The primary reason for that collapse must be attributed to adherence to a system of government that shut down virtually every semblance of a God-fearing religion, including its churches, synagogues, and mosques . . . a system that had no respect for a Supreme Being. Indeed, it was the threat of political condemnation, and possible sentencing to the Siberian gulags for any expression of God-fearing religion in opposition to Communist dictates, that caused the collapse of the "Evil Empire" and its subsequent ruin.

That collapse was inevitable regardless of what President Reagan may, or may not, have done. The Communist system, and its lack of regard for God, a Supreme Being, is what caused its predictable collapse. It would have happened with or without Reagan . . . maybe a little longer, but nevertheless inevitable. No nation can long survive without faith in, and respect for, the Creator and the Provider of all humanity. When that faith and respect is stifled or eliminated in any nation, its days as a viable governing entity are numbered.

History offers conclusive proof in the downfall of the Roman Empire, the Spanish Empire, the British Empire, and the Soviet Union.

The concerns that Dr. Kennedy expressed in 1984, and his prediction of what lay in store for America should it continue on the path of Humanism, have now been clearly validated. I need not repeat what has already been said herein, and in other venues, about the decline of morality in America . . . in virtually every aspect of our social, economic, and political order, including within traditional religious denominations themselves.

The so-called "economic boom" of the past seven years is the result of a "house of cards" (a.k.a. "an inflated stock market") constructed out of blue sky and quicksand. It is the product of a gambling craze and a virtual Ponzi scheme that defies all fundamentals, reality, common sense, and respect for moral ethics. When that bubble bursts, as it inevitably must, we will then be confronted with the dire consequences of the moral degradation of our society and its financial and political leadership.

It could happen only in a society that has been brainwashed for nearly fifty years to reject the religious principles propounded by our Founding Fathers.

We are on the same path, albeit slightly different and perhaps a little slower, than under the Communist regime of the Soviet Union, but we are, inexorably, on that path. No nation built on bread and circuses and blue sky, while rejecting time-honored principles of morality built on reverence for a Supreme Being, can avoid its ultimate downfall. Just like the Soviet Union.

The question that now confronts us is: "Are we willing to heed the warnings and restore our faith in the principles on which our nation was founded over 210 years ago, and how do we proceed to accomplish that restoration?"

Chapter 11 will offer a first and all-important step in answering that question.

11

Vouchers—
A Case for
Equal Protection

In preceding chapters we documented why an alarming number of government school graduates are ill-equipped to make responsible decisions concerning various aspects of our political, economic, and social order.

We documented why an antireligion culture is a product of an antireligion environment in government schools, caused by its adherence to the religion of Humanism, as propounded by John Dewey and the National Education Association.

And we documented how government has created an economic wall that makes it impossible for millions of parents to send their children to parochial schools, thereby denying them free exercise of religion as guaranteed by the First Amendment.

Finally, we indicted the State for violating not only the First Amendment of the U.S. Constitution, but also the equal protection clause of the Fourteenth Amendment, and the states rights provisions of the Tenth Amendment.

When Congress must stoop to debating the issue of same-sex marriages—and when our courts grant preferred rights to homosexuals over those who honor natural law and religious doctrine—it is proof positive that our nation has been in a state of moral, economic, and social decline.

Nor should it be surprising that all this has paralleled the steady closure of parochial schools, the degradation of moral and spiritual values in government-run schools, and the inability of a rising number of Americans to tell the difference between right and wrong in many issues.

When the products of government schools have no moral guideposts, subscribe to situation ethics, can't tell the difference between right and wrong, and are advised not to be judgmental, while relying on morally bankrupt movies and television, state-sponsored gambling, rock culture, drugs, and an economic system that has no regard for the laws or the people of any nation for their "inspiration," it should not be surprising that America is in serious trouble. The Honorable Judge Robert H. Bork, a strict interpreter of the Constitution, summed it up in the title of his book, *Slouching Toward Gomorrah*.

The Challenge

Now the challenge is: "What should be done about it? How do we get America back on the right path, the path laid out by the fifty-five men who met in Philadelphia in 1787?"

When weighed against this great challenge, debate about prayer in government schools, creationism vs. evolution, sovereignty vs. globalism, fundamentalism vs. Humanism, etc., pales into insignificance.

Vouchers—A Case for Equal Protection 143

☆ They are evasions from the infinitely more critical issue: "Should government continue to hinder and interfere with the free exercise of religion by imposing an economic wall, under the guise of free public education, that undermines Constitutional guarantees?"

If parents prefer that their children pray in school, or be taught academics tempered by moral principles embodied in religious teachings, they should not be subjected to debates in Congress, or in the media, that simply avoid facing up to the full meaning and intent of the First Amendment, and the manner in which the State has created policies that trample on the guarantees embodied therein.

☆ It warrants repeating: "Of what value is our Constitutional guarantee of free exercise of religion when the State takes away all, or any part, of its economic life-blood and uses it to create an economic wall that stands as an adversarial barrier to the fulfillment of that guarantee?"

Equal Access to Education Funds

Of course, it would be impractical, if not impossible, to reduce government taxation and interference in parental financial abilities to levels existing in 1787, or even forty years ago.

But that should not preclude granting to all parents, including those who prefer a religiously oriented education for their children, *equal* access to education funds. That would be consistent with the guarantee of free exercise of religion. To deny them that *equal* right relegates them to second-class citizens in violation of the equal protection clause of the Fourteenth Amendment, as well as the First Amendment.

☆ Current policies clearly discriminate against religion, contrary to what the First Amendment says and intends.

In a nutshell, all U.S. citizens, including parents who prefer that their children be educated in a religious environment, should be granted equal access to tax funds that belong to "We, the People" in the first place, rather than allocating such funds only to schools that function as adversaries against religion. That would be consistent with the equal protection clause of the Fourteenth Amendment, as well as the First Amendment.

Vouchers: The Key to Equality

The manner in which that can be done is simple. It would allow parents, on behalf of their children, to share on an equal basis in tax funds allocated to education, via a system commonly called "vouchers."

Such vouchers should have a uniform value, depending on state or local circumstances, between 80 percent and 100 percent of average per-pupil costs in public schools. They should be issued to parents, or guardians, on behalf of their children. They would then be given to school officials as payment of tuition at any school of their choice whether it be public, private secular, or parochial.

School personnel would then fill in the necessary information, such as name of child and parents or guardians, grade level, name and location of school, and other pertinent information, including certification signatures by school officials. The completed voucher would then be forwarded to appropriate government agencies who would issue a check to the parent or guardian for the full value of the voucher.

The parent or guardian would then endorse the voucher check and give it to the school of their choice. Thus, the action of the State is neutral. Parents and guardians make the final decision as to how the funds are disbursed.

Vouchers Go to Parents . . . Not Schools

It is important to understand that the voucher is payable to the parent or guardian, not to a specific school. In that way it avoids a direct link between the State and the school. The parent or guardian simply endorses the voucher/check over to the school of choice. In that manner, government "makes no law respecting an establishment of religion" . . . neither for nor against. It remains neutral.

- ☆ Parents are then free to "exercise their freedom of religion" by sending the child to a parochial school, or not to exercise that religious option by sending their child to a private secular or a public school.
- ☆ Should the State taint that voucher by denying its use at a parochial school, the State would then be "making a law respecting an establishment of religion" in a manner that is discriminatory and contrary to the free exercise and equal protection clauses.

U.S. Supreme Court Rules in Favor of Neutrality

This method of issuing vouchers to parents is clearly consistent with a U.S. Supreme Court ruling on June 28, 2000. In *Mitchell v. Helms*, the Supreme Court by a 6 to 3 margin ruled that so-called aid to parochial schools does not violate the Constitution if the funds involved are disbursed in a neutral manner. Here is a verbatim excerpt of that ruling, as written by Justice Clarence Thomas:

> "As part of the longstanding school aid program known as Chapter 2, the federal government distributes funds to state and local governmental agencies, which in turn lend educational materials and equipment to public and private schools, with the enrollment of each participating school determining the amount of aid it receives. The question is whether Chapter 2, as applied in Jefferson Parish, La., is a law respecting an establishment of religion, because many of the private

schools receiving Chapter 2 aid in that parish are religiously affiliated. We hold that Chapter 2 is not such a law.

☆ ☆ ☆

"Considering Chapter 2 in light of our more recent case law, we conclude that it neither results in religious indoctrination by the government nor defines its recipients by reference to religion. We therefore hold that Chapter 2 is not a 'law respecting and establishment of religion.'

☆ ☆ ☆

"As a way of assuring neutrality, we have repeatedly considered whether any governmental aid that goes to a religious institution does so 'only as a result of the genuinely independent and private choices of individuals.'

☆ ☆ ☆

"Private choice also helps guarantee neutrality by mitigating the preference for pre-existing recipients that is arguably inherent in any governmental aid program, and that could lead to a program inadvertently favoring one religion or favoring religious private schools in general over non-religious ones.

"Applying the two relevant Agostini criteria, we see no basis for concluding that Jefferson Parish's Chapter 2

Vouchers—A Case for Equal Protection 147

program 'has the effect of advancing religion.' Chapter 2 does not result in governmental indoctrination, because it determines eligibility for governmental aid neutrally, allocates the aid based on private choices of the parents of schoolchildren and does not provide aid that has an impermissible content. Nor does Chapter 2 define its recipients by reference to religion.

"Taking the second criterion first, it is clear that Chapter 2 aid 'is allocated on the basis of neutral, secular criteria that neither favor nor disfavor religion, and is made available to both religious and secular beneficiaries on a non-discriminatory basis.

"In short, Chapter 2 satisfies both the first and second primary criteria of Agostini. It therefore does not have the effect of advancing religion. For the same reason, Chapter 2 also 'cannot reasonably be viewed as an endorsement of religion.' Accordingly, we hold that Chapter 2 is not a law respecting an establishment of religion.

It should be apparent to any open-minded observer of the Supreme Court's ruling in *Mitchell v. Helms*, that the rationale used therein to determine allocation of government funds, which may or may not gravitate to parochial schools, is not a law respecting religion if the funds are disbursed in a neutral manner, i.e., letting the parent or guardian decide which school receives the funds.

To deny a similar parental option in the case of tuition vouchers would fly in the face of the Supreme Court's ruling. It would also violate the equal protection clause of the Fourteenth Amendment. Religiously oriented parents and their children would be relegated to second-class citizens. That would be not only highly discriminatory but also an unconscionable display of deliberate hostility to all things religious.

No Strings

Such vouchers should contain no "strings," except that schools should be accredited in basic academic curricula (such as reading, writing, mathematics, science, history, geography, and political sciences), with a firm understanding that parochial and private schools have *complete authority* to decide on *how* these subjects are taught and what textbooks are used.

The only other requirement is that the student should pass a test, to be determined by the school, before promotion to a higher grade or before a graduation diploma is awarded. The school would forward a notice to public officials when the student has completed the school term for which the voucher was issued. If the student "dropped out" before the end of the term the school would notify public officials accordingly and refund the unused portion of the voucher.

The State must adopt a hands-off stance in all other matters, including refraining from conducting audits of any kind into the internal affairs of private secular and parochial schools, or to require such schools to submit reports other than those mentioned above.

Obviously, public school hard-liners, especially the National Education Association and other special-interest unions and organizations, strenuously object to any voucher system. Even in the event that a voucher system is installed, they will still want to dictate the curricula and how subjects will be taught whether it be in private, parochial, or public schools, so as to achieve the goals of Karl Marx and John Dewey's *Humanist Manifesto*. But such intrusions should be banned!

As Cal Thomas wrote: "The humanist left knows the only way it can create substantial numbers of new ideological and social robots eager to follow in their failed footsteps is to imprison substantial numbers of children in government schools where they are force-fed liberal ideology and lied to about sex, about history, and about a lot of other things at taxpayer expense."

But restrictions against such intervention must be made a part of the transfer of education back to parents or guardians, in accordance with the U.S. Constitution.

Church and State

Such a voucher system should not be interpreted as a breach of "separation of church and state" theory, which as emphasized herein finds no support in the U.S. Constitution. Moreover, even if such a theory were valid, we should recognize that the State abrogated that theory long ago by its blatant intrusion into parental economic capabilities with regrettable impact on parochial schools, as well as the public school system, and our entire social, economic, and political order.

Let us be reminded again that the Constitution says nothing about "separation" of church and state. The Constitution does not say "freedom *from* religion." It says "freedom *of* religion" with emphasis on its positive aspects.

The Money Belongs to "We, the People"

Arguments that public funds should not be used in any way for education in a religious environment suggests that all money belongs to the State, when, in fact, the money was earned by, and belonged to, "We, the People" in the first place, and was confiscated via legalized plunder.

Any argument to the contrary suggests surrender to socialist or neocommunist systems that are being rejected throughout the world. The fall of the Communist Soviet Bloc was far more a result of the suppression of religious values than anything else.

Public school administrators, teachers, unions, atheists, agnostics, humanists, the ACLU, PAW, Barry Lynn, etc., are opposed to a voucher system in the same way that children are inclined to throw tantrums when their source of candy and other goodies is cut off. They have said a voucher system would "threaten, undermine, even destroy" the public school system. While such appraisals are highly debatable (many believe competition would vastly improve the quality of public education at far lower costs), that is beside the point.

> ☆ The objective of the public school establishment is clear. They seek to maintain a monopoly that restrains, restricts, and interferes with the availability of the "people's" funds for parochial and private secular schools because they know parochial and private secular schools are more productive, at far lower costs, and *they cannot stand that kind of competition.*

They have been so ingrained with the religion of Humanism in the public school system that they cannot, or do not want to, understand the meaning and intent of the Constitution.

The government school lobby has conspired to protect its own coercive monopoly to the detriment of parochial and private schools, and to the detriment of our nation as a whole. But there is nothing whatsoever in the U.S. Constitution that is even remotely aimed at protecting government-run schools to the detriment of any other school system or expression of religion.

To say the NEA has an intense hatred for religious schools would not be an overstatement. This is their policy platform, in keeping with John Dewey's *Humanist Manifesto* . . . and any threat to that policy is viewed as a threat to their jobs and monopoly.

More Court Decisions

We have already cited various Court decisions that have affirmed the Constitutionality of equal access to school funds for parochial schools. Here are two more:

On October 4, 1999, the U.S. Supreme Court refused to hear challenges to Arizona's tax credit plan that helps finance religious schools. It provides for up to a five-hundred-dollar tax credit for donations to "school tuition organizations," and up to two hundred dollars in additional tax credits for direct gifts for extracurricular activities. The Arizona program would generate $75 million a year for private schools, most of which are religiously oriented.

On November 4, 1998, the Justices refused to hear a review of a Wisconsin program that provides vouchers for up to five thousand dollars a year per child to attend private schools, most of which are parochial. Some eight thousand children already attend such schools.

Antireligion Claims Are Bogus and Inconsistent

The allegation that the State should not be involved in religion, or to permit expressions of God-fearing religion on public properties, flies in the face of widespread practices already in effect. Let's review some of them.

Contributions to churches are tax-deductible on income tax returns even though some of those funds are used to maintain schools that operate under the control of churches. Also, in all jurisdictions, churches are exempt from property and other taxes. Thus, government has already "made laws with respect to the free exercise of religion." So a voucher system that would be redeemable by a parochial school is not an earthshaking innovation.

Some diehard antireligion folks contend that such tax policies should be repealed . . . that churches should pay property taxes and individuals should not be granted a deduction for contributions to churches, or other religious organizations, on their tax returns. But if that concept were to be activated, government would then be "making a law respecting an establishment of religion" that would "restrain and interfere with the free exercise thereof," in violation of the First Amendment.

Contributions to religiously affiliated universities, such as Notre Dame, Boston College, the University of San Diego, Marquette, Southern Methodist, St. Mary's College, etc., are tax-deductible on income tax returns . . . even though students are taught in a religious environment and are encouraged to attend services in churches or chapels on university grounds. The prevailing view is that government cannot discriminate against religiously affiliated universities since it grants deductions on income tax returns for contributions to secular universities. To do otherwise would be discriminatory and contrary to guarantees in the First and Fourteenth Amendments.

An Anomaly

Property and school district taxes for the purpose of funding a government-run school system that millions of parents do not want *are* tax-deductible. Why then shouldn't parents be allowed to deduct tuitions paid to schools they *do* want?

That question poses an anomaly. If it is proper to exempt payments to churches that maintain elementary and/or secondary schools, and if it is proper to grant tax exemptions for contributions to universities that teach students in a religious environment, why should parents be denied the right to deduct from their income tax returns tuitions paid to church-run schools for their own children, especially since they are forced to pay taxes for public schools which *are* tax deductible . . . and which they *don't* want?

On the other hand, if a nonparent were to make a donation to a church-run K–12 school, it would qualify as a tax deduction on income tax returns. If that person were not granted that exemption, government would have "made a law respecting an establishment of religion," while simultaneously restraining and restricting "the free exercise of religion" in violation of the First Amendment.

There is a fine line constructed on a premise that a tax deduction is not allowable if the tuition is paid for the education of a parent's own child. Conversely, if a parent makes a donation to a church which uses that money, in total or in part, to educate the parent's child, but without specifying that the money be used by the school, the donation is tax deductible.

Here the tax code seems to be in conflict with itself and is, therefore, subject to charges of discrimination, especially in respect to the establishment and free exercise clauses.

The excuse has been offered that a tax deduction is not allowed if the payment is for tuition for the education of a parent's child on a premise that such tuitions are "for services rendered and value received." But that excuse is blatantly discriminatory inasmuch as payment of taxes to pay for the education of the parent's child at a public school, "for services rendered and value received," is tax deductible.

Moreover, the same excuse might be made that a donation to a church which the donor attends regularly is not tax deductible on a premise that it is for "spiritual services rendered." Thus, if such donations are tax deductible for adult/parents, why are they not also tax deductible for children of those parents? The "services rendered" excuse is bogus.

Parents Pay Taxes for Schools They Don't Want

As property owners, millions of people are forced by federal, state, and local laws to pay taxes to fund a government school system which, like Yoder, they do not want for their children. Those taxes are deductible on income tax returns. But, they want the right to "exercise freedom of religion" by sending their children to parochial schools for which they are required to pay tuitions of $3,000 to $5,000 a year after having already been forced to pay taxes to support schools they do not want. This is tantamount to double jeopardy.

Although parents get a deduction for taxes paid to fund public schools they do not want, they are not allowed a deduction for tuitions to educate their children in a parochial school, even though they have relieved the State of the cost of educating their child . . . at a savings to the State of about $6,000 each.

It would seem that the State would rush to welcome such an arrangement. At the 28 percent federal tax bracket, a tax deduction of $4,000 for tuition at a parochial school would reduce government tax revenue by only $1,120 while saving $6,000 for not having to educate a child. The State would save $4,880 in the process . . . a very good deal for public schools, and taxpayers.

The Real Reason

Why wouldn't they approve such a plan? The obvious reason, of course, is that the government school monopoly, ruled by antireligion people, has put its foot down on anything that smacks of belief in God . . . anything that stands in the way of fulfilling the agenda of the *Humanist Manifesto* . . . and anything that would inject competition into the education of children. It is pure, unadulterated discrimination and a violation of the letter and spirit of the First and Fourteenth Amendments.

Social Security and Medicare

The U.S. Social Security and Medicare programs are funded by a FICA tax (currently 15.3 percent on wages) for the purpose of paying pensions to retirees, as well as hospital and medical care.

In the case of hospital and medical, these "public" funds are then disbursed to sectarian as well as secular institutions. Many hospitals are owned and operated by religious institutions where members of the cloth minister to ailing people and say prayers with them. Although government checks are issued directly to such religiously affiliated institutions for the care of sick people, no one is suggesting that this constitutes a violation of "separation of church and state" theories. Why then is there opposition to disbursing so-called "public funds" to religiously affiliated schools for the education of children?

The only logical conclusion is that the public school monopoly is committed to the continued indoctrination of children into the Humanist religion of Dewey and Marx so that when children become adults they will be advocates of the same socialist, neocommunist system in which they were brainwashed.

Similarly, government issues checks from "public funds" for "Social Security pensions" to many individuals who endorse those checks over to retirement homes owned and operated by religious institutions that provide religious services for their tenants, including the right to pray in group sessions. Why then should there be any objection to a voucher system whereby checks are drawn against "public funds" to parents who then endorse those checks over to a school of their choice?

The obvious answer to these questions is that the State has caved in to the NEA lobby, in violation of the establishment, free exercise, and equal protection clauses.

Clearly, the policy of government in the case of education vs. Medicare and Social Security is flagrantly inconsistent and discriminatory. It reflects a commitment to the Marx/Dewey agenda that children must be indoctrinated into a "One-World Social Order" so they become its docile supporters when they become adults, including submission to a global economy that has no regard for the laws or the people of any nation.

They are saying that it is okay to use public funds for elderly people, but such funds should not be used to indoctrinate children with religious beliefs for fear that when they become adults they would oppose the neocommunist agenda of the *Humanist Manifesto,* and certain government policies, such as abortions, homosexuality, unwarranted military aggressions, advancement of global socialism, redistribution-of-wealth tax codes, etc.

More Inconsistencies

One of the crown jewels of the post–World War II era, the GI Bill, was basically a voucher program for education. Returning veterans could go to any college of their choosing, including Notre Dame and Southern Methodist. No one saw this as a sinister scheme to violate the separation of church and state. Instead, Americans saw it as a way to create a better society, and they were right. What is it, then, about parochial schools for children that sends otherwise rational people into a tizzy? Surely, it is not concern for students and a better society. The goal of the public school monopoly is to brainwash children in their formative years so they will yield to the amoral religion of Humanism when they become adults.

Government pays for religious chaplains in Congress and at most military establishments. Indeed, on the grounds of the Air Force Academy in Colorado Springs, government, at the expense of taxpayers at large, built one of the most beautiful churches in America, and staffed it with clergy.

Whereas the Ten Commandments have been banned from any display in public schools, district court rooms, and other public properties, they are engraved on the walls of the U.S. Supreme Court building.

Every session of Congress is opened with a prayer by a tax-paid chaplain. The Bible is used in the swearing-in ceremonies of the president, cabinet members, and members of Congress.

Our currency is inscribed with the words "In God We Trust," yet parents are not allowed to entrust their children to a school that professes a belief in God.

Every year the president turns on a switch to light the national Christmas Tree in honor of the birth of Christ. Yet, Christmas trees and other displays honoring the birth of Christ are not permitted on many public grounds on a specious premise that they are religious symbols in violation of the separation of church and state.

The only conclusion we can draw from all this is that the antireligious lobby—consisting of the government school establishment, liberal politicians beholden to Marx/Dewey socialist theology, and an antireligion liberal media—have drawn a line in the sand in total disregard of the U.S. Constitution.

With a closed mind they have said: "Under no circumstance will any religious view or symbol be allowed on public property . . . that such property is only for the purpose of advancing the religion of Humanism. We don't want any interference from any other religion or your sectarian morals." But they have no Constitutional authority to adopt such policies.

Diversity

Over forty years ago, in 1957, I wrote: "Woe be the day that our elementary and public school system is run from the top down . . . that its curricula and objectives are determined by the federal government." I said it would be a prescription for the gradual "mind-control indoctrination" of America's children for the benefit of devious politicians and their sycophants in much the same way that Hitler and Stalin came to power.

I said then that one of the great things about our educational system was its "diversity." It is rather ironic, therefore, that just as our political leaders now speak about "diversity" as it relates to the ethnic and sexual diversity of our culture, they condemn diversity in education if it relates to moral principles emanating from God-fearing religion.

The Department of Education Should Be Shut Down

One of worst things that ever happened to the education of children is the formation of a federal Department of Education. It should be abolished! The education of our children should be returned to local school boards and parents as the Constitution stipulated in the Tenth Amendment.

Article I, Section 8 of the Constitution lists eighteen areas in which Congress and the federal government may be involved. Public education is not one of them. Such federal programs as Outcome-Based Education (OBE) and Goals 2000 are without Constitutional authority. They intrude on the great potential of diversity in our schools, while being at odds with a brand of diversity promoted by social engineers who favor diversity only if it helps to achieve their amoral goals.

Sadly, we have departed from the virtue of diversity in our educational system, even as some cry for diversity in sexual behavior. Instead of diversity in education, we have been forced to yield to a top-down tyranny that is the precursor of one-world socialism, in which the freedoms of American citizens are being transferred to a small group of powerful elites in the financial and political sectors. Like all top-down systems (such as in the former Soviet Union), it is doomed to failure from the very outset.

☆ ☆ ☆
In Conclusion

☆ The First Amendment of the U.S. Constitution was adopted to protect and guarantee the free exercise of religion, not public schools!

A burglar who steals any part of your possessions is guilty of stealing. To no lesser degree, a government that steals *any* part of the financial means to freely exercise religion, and then uses that money to maintain an amoral public school system, while denying equal access to such funds by those who want their children educated in a religious environment, is guilty of stealing our First and Fourteenth Amendment rights.

☆ By creating an economic system that is effectively closing down religious schools and restraining parental ability to perpetuate their religious beliefs in their children, the State is guilty of violating the Constitution of the United States.

☆ The State should stop such violations forthwith!

☆ It is time to restore the liberties for which our forefathers so gallantly fought . . . for the moral and spiritual First Amendment rights of "We, the People," to send our children to the schools of our choice.

☆ That objective can be accomplished only by means of a voucher system that would provide "We, the People" *an equal protection share* of funds that belonged to us in the first place!

MAY GOD BLESS AMERICA!

☆ ☆ ☆

Index

A

Abortions, 4
ACLU, American Civil Liberties Union, 66, 71, 74, 83, 92, 126, 150
Adams, President John, 79
Adversarial Role of Public Schools, 106–122
American Humanist Association, 61, 63
America On Line Poll (Football Case), 129, 130
Americans United For Separation of Church & State, 66, 71
Apathy, Public, 51, 52
Arizona Tax Credit Plan, 152
Author, 171

B

Bastiat, Frederic, 24, 25, 31, 64, 107, 130
Black, Justice Hugo, 68
Bork, Judge Robert, 72, 142
Boston Tea Party, 112
Bowles, Linda, 55–57
Brennan, Justice William, 51
Bumpers, Senator Dale, 16
Buchanan, Pat, 19
Burger, Chief Justice Warren, 51
Burglary Analogy, 107, 108, 159

C

Carter, President Jimmy, 75, 78, 139
Catholic Schools, 120

Chaplains
  In Congress, 128, 156
  In Military Establishments, 157
Challenge, The Key, 142
Child Care, 32, 33
Christian Coalition, 85, 86
Christianity, United States Founded On, 72
Christmas Trees, 157
Clinton, Hillary Rodham, 101
Clinton, President William J., 3, 16–19
Collins, Bertram F., 69
Columbine High School Massacre, 6, 7, 82
Communist Manifesto, 28, 40, 104, 126
Conclusion, 159
Condoms, Distribution of, 5
Court Cases:
  Cantwell v State of Connecticut, 88
  Engels v. Vitale, 73
  Lamb's Chapel v Center Moriches School Dist., 74, 76
  Mitchell v Helms – Aid to Public Schools, 145–147
  Rosenberger v Rector and Univ. of VA, 74, 76
  Sherbert v Verner, 114
  Sante Fe Schools District v Jane Doe, 123–130
  State of Maine, 115
  Torcaso v Watkins, 68, 69, 137
Constitution Issues—Humanism as a Religion, 69, 70
Constitution—Article 1, Sec. 1 & 8, 22
Constitution, Commentaries on, 95, 96
Currency, U.S., 98, 157

D

Danbury Baptist Association, 77, 78, 94
Declaration of Independence, 62, 72
Debt, Federal, 52, 53, 110

Index **163**

DeKalb County, Alabama, 100, 101
Denver v. Reiter, 82
Dewey, John, 18, 28, 29, 30, 32, 40, 49, 58, 59, 60, 66, 69, 70, 72, 104, 105, 108, 113, 114, 119, 125, 137, 148, 150, 155
Discrimination, 2, 3, 17
Diversity, 157, 158
Dobson, Dr. James, 19
Douglas, Justice William O., 101
Dunphy, John, 63
Drug Culture, 9, 10

E

Economics of Religion, 105–122
Economic Wall, 145
Education, Federal Dept. of, 159
Education, Public, 22
Ellerbee, Linda, 21, 39, 58
Equal Access, 143, 144
Equal Protection Clause—14th Amendment, 30, 70, 73, 75, 81, 113, 114
Establishment Clause—1st Amendment, 73, 80, 81, 83, 84, 92, 126, 128, 129
Encyclopedia of Religion in American Politics, 66, 67, 75
Etowah County, Alabama, 89

F

Falwell, Rev. Jerry, 86
Feinstein, Senator Dianne, 16
First Amendment, 22, 23, 67, 70, 71–88, 92, 124, 132, 133
First Amendment, Purpose of, 85
Football Case, 123–130
Foreign Trade, 11–13, 18, 33, 109, 110, 111

Fortkamp, Dr. Frank E., 44
Free Exercise Clause—1st Amendment, 75, 80, 81, 83, 84, 87, 88, 106–108, 125, 127, 143, 145
Free Speech Clause—1st Amendment, 73, 74, 87, 88, 108, 125

G

G-I Bill, 156
Government Interferes with Free Exercise, 143

H

Henry, Patrick, 103
Hillsdale College, 89
Hippocratic Oath, 5
Historical Precedents, 97
Hitler, Adolf, 2, 64, 69, 157
HIV/AIDS, 3, 15
Hoagland, Nebraska State Senator Peter, 119
Hoffman, Dustin, 9
Hollywood, 8
Homosexuals and Lesbians, 3
House of Cards, 141
Humanist Manifesto, 28, 30, 40, 59, 70, 104, 113, 114, 125, 137, 148, 150, 154, 156
Humanism as a Religion, 60–65, 138, 156
Humanism, Evolution of, 66, 67
Humanism, Secular, 66, 134

I

Impeachment, 10
"Import Schools from Japan, Too", 40–43, 46, 47
Indoctrination of Children, 26
Inflation, 109
"It's Elementary", 3

Index

J
Jefferson, President Thomas, 62, 72, 79, 94–96, 134
Johnson, President Lyndon Baines, 36
Judicial Activism, 103, 104
Judicial System, 13, 14, 50, 51

K
Kennedy, Dr. D. James, 4, 131–140
Kervorkian, Dr. Jack, 5

L
Last Supper (Judas), 115
Legalized Theft, 24, 25, 113, 130
Leland, Rev. John, 95
Locke, John, 94
Lynn, Barry, 74, 115, 116, 150

M
Madison, President James, 79, 95, 96, 135
Marx, Karl, 19, 28, 32, 33, 39, 40, 58, 72, 104, 105, 119, 126, 148, 155
McCain, Senator John, 19
Mill, John Stuart, 45
Milosevic, Slobodan, 18
Money Belongs to "We, The People", 149, 159
Moore, Judge Roy S., 89–104
Moore, Rev. E. Ray, 34
Morality, Legislating, 134

N
National Education Association (NEA), 27, 30, 37, 40, 66, 68, 70, 114, 115, 125, 126, 148, 150

"Nation at Risk" Report, 57
Nightmare of Camelot, 34

O

O'Connor, Justice Sandra Day, 54, 87, 123

P

Packwood, Senator Robert, 22
People for the American Way (PAW), 66, 71, 150
"Petition of Government" Clause—1st Amendment, 75
Pledge of Allegiance, 48
Prayer, National Day of, 51
Public Property, Use of, 127
Public Schools
   Founded on, 24
   Plunder and Legalized Theft, 24, 25
   Karl Marx Socialism, 24
   Communist Manifesto, 24
   John Dewey's Humanist Manifesto, 242
   America's Biggest Welfare Program, 24
   In a Moral Vacuum, 24, 49

R

Reagan, President Ronald, 138–140
Reed, Ralph, 86
Religion, Definitions of, 68
Religion, What Qualifies As, 67
Rehnquist, Chief Justice William, 15, 74, 86, 98, 124
Responsibility, Sexual, 37–39
Revolutionary War, 23
Robertson, Pat, 86
Roman Empire, 102

Index

S

Salaries, Teacher, 27
  vs. Japan, 42, 43
Scalia, Justice Antonin, 87, 124
Secular Humanism, 66, 134
Separation of Church and State Myth, 77, 78, 124
Seattle Post-Intelligencer, 10, 21
Seattle Public Schools, 119, 120
Sexual Promiscuity, 4, 5, 53, 54
Shearer, William K., 7, 8
Simpson, O.J., 13
Skullduggery in Congress and Boardrooms, 10
Smoot, Dan, 45
Socialism, 30–32
  Global, 30–33
Social Security/Medicare, 155
Sodomy, 53
Soviet Communism, 136, 138–149
Spending Up, Quality Down, 121
Stalin, Josef, 2, 64, 157
States vs. Christianity
  Alabama, 92
  California, 91
  Kansas, 91
  Ohio, 92
State as a Giant Adversary, 112–114
State vs. America, 119
State Violates First Amendment, 122
States Rights—10th Amendment 22, 159
Stephanopolis, George, 3
Stevens, Justice John Paul, 123, 124, 126, 127, 130
Stewart, Justice Potter, 100
Story, Justice Joseph, 96, 101
Supreme Court, 97
  1962, New York Board of Regents, 94

Santa Fe Football Case, 123–130
  Building, 156
Survey, Car Buyers, 41, 42

T

Tax Deductions, Contributions to Churches, 152
  Tuition, 152–154
  Universities, 152
Taxation and Inflation, 108, 109
Tax Dippers, 40
Taxes, 25, 26, 108
  Property, 152, 153, 155
  School District, 152
Ten Commandments, 6, 39, 85, 92, 93, 102, 135, 156
Tenth Amendment, 22, 159
Thomas, Cal, 148, 149
  Justice Clarence, 124, 145
Tolerance, 4
Tuition, 152, 153

U

United Nations, 16
U.S. Constitution, a Binding Contract, 77, 78
U.S. Currency—"In God We Trust", 98, 156
U.S. Declares War on Parochial Schools, 120

V

Valenti, Jack, 10
Vaudeville Routine, 124
Violence in Schools, 6, 7, 118
Voltaire, 4
Vouchers, 143–160
  Go To Parents, 144, 145

Key to Equality, 144
No Strings Attached, 148, 149
State of Maine Plan, 115
State of Wisconsin Plan, 151

W

Washington, President George, 17, 18, 30, 78, 91, 97, 135
Wealth, Origin of, 24, 25
Welfare Program, 35, 36
Whitman, Governor Christine, 15
Wilson, Governor Pete, 37

Y

Yeltsin, Boris, 139
Yoder vs. Wisconsin, 118, 153
Yugoslavia and Kosovo, Bombing of, 17–19

About the Author

Gus Stelzer was born June 1, 1915, in St. Louis, the second child in a poor family of six children. He graduated from a Lutheran parochial school at the age of twelve after being promoted twice to higher grades. Lacking a steady family income his parents could not afford to send him through high school. Using money earned in various sales ventures he paid his own tuition at the Missouri Business School for an eighteen-month course in speed math, accounting, commercial law, typing, and other business principles, graduating at the age of fourteen in September 1929.

One month later the Crash of October 1929 made history, thereby triggering the Great Depression of the 1930s. His father was again unemployed. Young Stelzer found a job after two months of diligent search, as the accountant for a furniture manufacturer with twenty-eight employees, at ten dollars for a forty-eight-hour week. He was the only wage earner in a family of eight. At age seventeen, Stelzer became a sales representative for thirty auto parts manufacturers in a five-state area out of St. Louis.

In February 1935, Stelzer, then nineteen, was hired by the Zone Sales Office of the Chevrolet Division, General Motors Corp. In the subsequent forty-one years he was promoted twenty-three times, including transfers to twelve different locations throughout the U.S., including four years in the Detroit home office, from 1947 to 1951, where he had coresponsibility for rebuilding a retail sales organization of six thousand dealers, ten thousand managers and thirty-five thousand salesmen, which had been virtually depleted during World War II when auto production ceased.

In 1966 he achieved Senior Executive rank in General Motors, from which level he retired in mid-1976. In his last full year with GM he was in charge of over one thousand GM dealers and thirty-five thousand employees, doing $2 billion in annual sales in 1975 dollars.

He attributes the success not to being "smarter," but to the moral principles of the Ten Commandments that were embedded in his mind and conscience during his formative years while attending a parochial school. He earned a reputation for impeccable honesty and integrity, which earned the loyalty and all-out support of his subordinates, dealers, and other business associates, in every assignment. This, in turn, resulted in record sales, market penetration, and dealer profits.

Since 1976 Stelzer has been a member of the World Affairs Council; the Institute of the Americas at the University of California, San Diego; the Advisory Board of the School of Education at the University of San Diego; president of the Rotary Club of Rancho Santa Fe, California; plus many community activities, while maintaining constant study and involvement in matters of economics, foreign trade, and social issues.

He is the author of over 130 articles that have appeared in the public press, plus several books including *The Nightmare of Camelot,* which documents why U.S. trade policies are immoral, unconstitutional, and economic demagoguery. Since early 1995, he has appeared for one to three hours on 130 radio and TV talk shows, and before 135 audiences, as large as 800, from which he frequently received standing ovations.

He now resides in Mill Creek, Washington, with Lorraine, his wife of sixty years. They have a daughter and a son—both graduates of parochial schools and colleges, and with very successful business careers—plus seven grandchildren and two great-grandchildren.

—February 2000